International Monetary Reform, 1964-69

PRAEGER SPECIAL STUDIES IN
INTERNATIONAL ECONOMICS AND DEVELOPMENT

International Monetary Reform, 1964-69

THE POLITICAL DIMENSION

Stephen D. Cohen

PRAEGER PUBLISHERS
New York • Washington • London

The purpose of Praeger Special Studies is to make specialized research in U.S. and international economics and politics available to the academic, business, and government communities. For further information, write to the Special Projects Division, Praeger Publishers, Inc., 111 Fourth Avenue, New York, N.Y. 10003.

PRAEGER PUBLISHERS
111 Fourth Avenue, New York, N.Y. 10003, U.S.A.
5, Cromwell Place, London S.W.7, England

Published in the United States of America in 1970
by Praeger Publishers, Inc.

Library of Congress Catalog Card Number: 72-119521

Printed in the United States of America

TO LINDA

ACKNOWLEDGMENTS

On January 1, 1970, the International Monetary Fund allocated to its members history's first deliberately created international reserve asset, special drawing rights. This event marks the first structural change in the international monetary system created after World War II and represents the culmination of six years of effort by the Fund and the economic officials of the free world's major industrial countries. It is the background and meaning of monetary reform which form the substance of this volume.

When I started to research the very recent financial diplomacy which preceded this event, it became readily apparent that my efforts might have been totally frustrated by the official silence which surrounded the confidential monetary reform talks were it not for the numerous off-the-record interviews which participants subsequently granted me. It is therefore more than simple courtesy to express great appreciation to those officials in the International Monetary Fund and in the U.S. Government, especially my former Treasury Department colleagues, who so extensively discussed this subject with me. I am indebted to Theodore A. Couloumbis, Frank M. Tamagna, and James H. Weaver, professors at the American University, for their editorial assistance and suggestions.

I also wish to acknowledge the encouragement and support, offered without any assumption of responsibililty for the substance of my text, that was extended by my colleagues at the United States-Japan Trade Council. Of course, this study represents only my personal interpretations and has no connection with my present or former employers. Responsibility for any errors of commission or omission that remain is mine.

Appreciation for my wife's interest, patience, and typing skills cannot be easily verbalized. It is conveyed in part by the dedication of this book.

S. D. C.

Washington, D.C.

CONTENTS

xi

LIST OF ABBREVIATIONS

BIS	Bank for International Settlements
CEA	Council of Economic Advisers
CRU	Composite Reserve Unit
EEC	European Economic Community
GAB	General Arrangements to Borrow
IMF	International Monetary Fund
IRF	International Reserve Fund
NATO	North Atlantic Treaty Organization
OECD	Organization for Economic Cooperation and Development
SDR's	Special Drawing Rights
SRDR	Special Reserve Drawing Rights

INTRODUCTION

To paraphrase Talleyrand's classic admonition on war and military men, the international monetary system is too complex a thing to be left to economists. Nevertheless, discussions of the functions and problems of the gold-exchange standard (so named because of its basic reliance on gold and reserve currencies), as well as the need to reform it, have generally been written by economists and couched in strictly economic terms. International finance no doubt is an esoteric subject in which a political scientist might seem to be out of place at best, or useless at worst. But what happens to the theory and laws of economics when they cross national boundaries? More often than not, they are confronted and reshaped by a superior force--national sovereignty and all of the trappings and foibles that go with this persistent fact of life in world politics.

The international monetary system was created and is maintained by independent nation-states. It works not by natural law but by the combined will of these states. Its successes and shortcomings are intimately affected by the political objectives, interests, and attitudes of these same states. When the system reaches a point where the economically powerful states feel that it must be reformed, both political and economic forces are responsible. This situation notwithstanding, the subjects of international finance in general and international monetary reform in particular have been virtually ignored by political scientists. Most economists writing in this field tend to attach no great significance to these political forces, partly because they are not as readily identifiable and quantifiable as are the inherent economic aspects of the subject, and partly because academic economists tend to think above the level of political expediency. The consequences of this situation is that the political elements of the recently completed international monetary reform exercise have all too often been discounted or ignored altogether.

Almost obscured by a proliferation of theoretical literature discussing the weaknesses of the monetary system and expounding on desirable structural reforms, a series of official talks made an unheralded start at the end of 1963 to inquire into the ability of the system to adequately serve the future needs of the world economy. Multilateral discussions of monetary arrangements and institutions are nothing new in the twentieth century. Two world wars and a depression have created the frequent need for multilateral consultations on possible changes in these institutions and arrangements. Hence, the series of monetary reform talks which began in 1963 represented another chapter in the evolution of that system.

The 1963 reform talks coincided almost exactly with the reform talks of 1958, a year which has come to represent the first major turning point in the postwar monetary system. Throughout 1958, a number of significant financial developments occurred. After a single year of surplus, the U.S. balance of payments began its so-called second generation of annual deficits which then continued unabated through 1967. In 1958, most of the Western European countries had experienced sufficient economic recovery to initiate a number of liberalization measures that included restoration of full currency convertibility for import and export (current account) transactions. The Treaty of Rome became effective in that year, and the European Economic Community (EEC)--the so-called Common Market-- officially came into existence. It was also in 1958 that Charles de Gaulle returned to power in France. By the end of the year, he had initiated what quickly proved to be a very effective program of economic stablilization.

As Europe increasingly developed economic strength and acquired U.S. dollars, the ground rules of the so-called gold-exchange standard began slowly but surely to change. The dollar shortage which had characterized international finance since World War II gradually evolved into a dollar glut after 1958. The continental countries had become chronic surplus countries and began to accumulate unwanted balances of dollars, much of which were sent back to the United States in exchange for gold. And as the U.S. payments deficit persisted, so too did its gold losses. With rapidly growing monetary reserves, the Europeans felt less and less disposed to extend unlimited credit to the United States as unflinchingly as had been done during this country's first generation of payments deficits. The latter was a welcome source of dollar reserves from 1950 through 1956. But in the 1960's, the dollar drain was a target of European political and economic criticism.

It has been suggested that there is a basic absurdity in a monetary system which, while highly dependent on the availability of reserve currencies to augment gold in monetary reserves, threatens to unravel if so much of these currencies is made available that doubts about exchange-rate stability begin. Because of what certain key countries looked upon as a surfeit of dollars, the economic powers of the Atlantic community officially agreed that the U.S. balance-of-payments deficit would have to be terminated. Simple arithmetical logic then indicated that a growing world economy would not be properly serviced by a monetary system about to denude itself of its primary source of new international liquidity (which, consisting of gold, reserve currencies, and access to such international credit facilities as the International Monetary Fund, may be defined as all of the resources unconditionally available to national monetary authorities to finance deficits in their country's balance of payments). Ergo, the system had to be reformed.

Unfettered by political considerations, academic and private economists devised detailed and workable proposals in a matter of weeks. But it took the financial diplomats more than four years to devise a viable and acceptable reserve asset to supplement gold and reserve currencies. Since one can dismiss the possibility of gross technical incompetence or indifference, there is only one valid explanation of the need for the seemingly interminable talks. The work of the financial diplomats was made exceedingly complex by their need to resolve a two-dimensional problem, one containing both political and economic elements. They had to produce an asset that was politically acceptable as well as economically viable. The level of international liquidity--or credit--that is available, as well as who controls its creation, is a political issue because it touches directly on the ability of sovereign states to pursue certain chosen policies and to affect the policies of other states.

The central thesis of this book is that the international monetary reform exercise of the mid 1960's, when viewed in a broad perspective, was ultimately political in nature. In other words, essential economic considerations were overwhelmed by the traditional process of politics--the striving to enhance various subjective values amidst a climate of varying shades of disagreement. In this sense, the amalgam of financial terms and concepts associated with the reform talks become recognizable as paralleling other aspects of Atlantic community politics. The dynamics and conflicts endemic to the North Atlantic area, especially the relationship of the United States to a resurgent Western Europe, gave birth to and guided the development of the international monetary reform talks.

The contemporary international monetary system, no less than the North Atlantic Treaty Organization (NATO), performed remarkably well as long as the political milieu in which it was created remained essentially unchanged. Both the monetary and the security systems of the Atlantic community were products of the immediate postwar period, a time of U.S. hegemony and European impotence. When, in the late 1950's, European political, economic, and military strength had been restored, the postwar power relationship between the United States and Western Europe moved slowly into obsolescence. As part of this process, Europeans became dissatisfied with the old monetary order and challenged some of its basic characteristics. The absence of a European-U.S. consensus on economic strategy and political objectives made necessary the establishment of a structurally modified international monetary system.

Whereas previous literature in this field has tended to treat the problem as one dimensional (economic), this study introduces politics as the all-important second dimension. The differentiation of relevant economic and political factors is a difficult but necessary task. In trying to make

such a distinction, it is necessary to first note
that the immediate end of international liquidity
is singularly technical--the temporary financing,
by expending gold and foreign exchange, of a
balance-of-payments deficit while the deficit
country's monetary authorities adjust domestic and
international economic policies to constrain international liabilities, e.g., imports, and to encourage international assets, e.g., exports. Obviously,
the more liquidity available to a nation under our
system of fixed exchange rates, the less the impact
of adjustment on domestic growth objectives. A
second purely technical factor was that of confidence. Once surplus countries began to fear the
ability of the United States to end its external
deficits, there was a resulting tendency on their
part to defer continued dollar accumulations and to
prefer holding some other asset, especially gold,
which has a minimal downside risk. The adjustment
and confidence factors are two straightforwardly
technical considerations, fully explainable in
terms of textbook economics.

From here on in, the waters become muddy as
the political strains flow in and dilute the formula. In other seemingly technical issues, such
as the need for discipline in maintaining balance-
of-payments equilibrium (by the Anglo-Saxon countries) and how far in advance of an actual expectation of a liquidity shortage negotiation of a new
asset should take place (i.e., before or after the
end of the U.S.-payments deficit), the vagaries
of international politics are already evident.
Once the monetary negotiations were actually underway, however, technical issues became virtually
nonexistent. Maneuvering along clearly recognizable
political lines, not on the basis of econometric
models, became prevalent. Maximization of politically induced value ends directly related to over-
all national interests meant that important
decisions in the monetary reform talks invariably
were made at the cabinet level or higher, not on
a professorial basis by a group of objective, technical experts sitting at the negotiating table.
The need to reconcile liquidity policies with the
wider range of national policies created the larger,
political dimension of international monetary
reform.

In order to prove that economic concepts and terminology are insufficient to explain the background, progression, and outcome of the international monetary reform exercise, a number of questions must be resolved. The first question is why can't the one right amount of international liquidity be computed and distributed accordingly? Once this question is resolved, a vacuum develops into which rush political forces, but why should this critically important reaction occur? Why and how do the dynamics of international politics concern themselves with such a seemingly straightforward technical issue as the international monetary system?

With the advent of the actual monetary reform talks, a further set of questions arises. In what ways did the antithetical United States and French positions and the German position, which is a synthesis of those of Germany's two most important allies, react with each other? In what ways are these three critical monetary policies rooted in the national interests of each country? How did the absence of an Atlantic political community but the presence of the EEC predisposition for unity affect the dynamics of the negotiations? What were the roles and policies of the other Group-of-Ten countries? Also, how did the less developed countries and international organization (the International Monetary Fund) affect the course of monetary talks which in previous years had been, and which in 1963 started out to be, a private preserve of the great powers?

The final question concerns the outcome of the talks: What was the relationship between a political struggle by Europe to achieve parity with the United States in the international monetary decisionmaking process and the nature of the special drawing rights agreement? How did the end product of the talks satisfy the political motivation underlying it?

International
Monetary Reform,
1964-69

CHAPTER **1** ECONOMIC AND
POLITICAL
CROSSCURRENTS

Once it can be shown that the "right amount" of
international liquidity is a totally subjective concept without a precise definition, a technical
vacuum is created into which flow the political
elements of international monetary affairs. This
chapter examines the limits of economics and the
beginnings of politics.

THE ECONOMICS OF
INTERNATIONAL LIQUIDITY

International liquidity is comprised of gold-
and foreign-exchange reserves and the access to
credit facilities such as the International Monetary
Fund (IMF). National monetary authorities accumulate and maintain liquidity in order to compensate
for the differential between the country's total
foreign-exchange receipts and total foreign-exchange
expenditures. It is in this way that IMF member
countries (which include almost all non-Communist
countries) maintain their formal commitment to
avoid fluctuations in their currency's rate of exchange of more than 1 percent in either direction.
Fixed exchange rates are the very heart of the gold-
exchange standard. They have introduced an element
of stability, predictability, and confidence into
the international monetary system, and this in turn
related to the unprecedented economic growth which
the free world has experienced since the end of
World War II.

World trade is financed on a day-to-day basis
by banks and credit institutions via the foreign-
exchange markets. It is only when a country's

aggregate international payments exceed receipts
that the overflow of its national currency on the
exchange market must be redeemed indirectly through
gold sales or directly with convertible foreign
exchange (primarily dollars) to avoid a depreciation
in its exchange rate. Such intervention restores
an equilibrium in the international supply of and
demand for a given currency. In the case of a
surplus country, its local currency is sold by the
central bank in return for gold and foreign exchange
to avoid an appreciation in its exchange rate.

The need for and use of international liquidity
are thus inherently technical in nature. Its phys-
ical use is dictated by purely quantitative factors,
and its immediate purpose is simply to permit a
country to make necessary economic adjustments in
a slow, orderly, and relatively painless manner.
But, like everything else in economics, the supply
of international reserves on an aggregate basis is
scarce relative to demand. Unless a country owns
unlimited reserves or has a reserve currency which
other countries want an unlimited amount of (as
was the case of the United States in the early
1950's), any protracted deficit will necessitate
adoption of remedial, growth-retarding economic
policies to restrict domestic spending and/or to
promote payments equilibrium by discouraging mer-
chandise imports and capital exports.

This situation poses a fundamental dilemma for
the international monetary system: Just how much
liquidity is enough? What volume of liquidity will
obviate the need for countries to adopt deflationary
"shock-treatments" in an effort to restore balance-
of-payments equilibria?

This problem is not new. In 1943, John Maynard
Keynes was considering exactly the same problem
confronting the monetary planners of the 1960's.
He wrote that the monetary system needed an amount
of international money neither determined in an
unpredictable and irrelevant manner as, for example,
by the technical progress of the gold industry, nor
subject to large variations depending on the gold-
reserve policies of individual countries; rather,
it should be governed by the actual current requirements of world commerce and be capable of deliberate
expansion and contraction to offset deflationary and
inflationary tendencies in effective world demand.

Economists have never been successful in agreeing on the optimal level of reserves. Robert Triffin put the dilemma in these terms:

> There is certainly a very wide range
> of actual reserve levels which might
> be regarded as satisfactory, or
> acceptable by the monetary authori-
> ties and which would not induce them
> to modify their policies in such a
> way as to sacrifice other and more
> fundamental policy goals, such as
> desirable rates of employment and
> economic growth, price stability,
> etc.[1]

In their first liquidity study, economic officials of the West's ten leading industrial countries admitted they knew of "no satisfactory quantitative formula" to measure international liquidity needs.

Increments in international trade do not seem to have any statistical correlation to increases in international liquidity. Historically, the proportion of liquidity to trade has varied, and no one has demonstrated any recurring ratio. Between 1958 and 1967, for example, the volume of trade doubled to approximately $200 billion, while liquidity increased by just a little more than 25 percent ($57-$73 billion).

The general consensus of the literature is that an increased volume of international economic intercourse in the years ahead will generate more severe payments deficits. Hence, large increments to the existing volume of international liquidity will be necessary to allow sufficient time for the preferred and acceptable measures of adjustment to take full effect and to prevent a relative scarcity of reserves from forcing countries to adopt restrictive policies and odious exchange controls or to devalue their currencies.

The all-important question of how much liquidity is enough defies a "right" answer, suggests Fritz Machlup, Director of Princeton's International Finance Section, because the level of reserves desired by central bankers is a normative matter shaped by such forces as tradition, fashion, and doctrine. No fixed amount of reserves can reasonably or scientifically be judged as being needed or adequate to prevent policymakers in a deficit country from imposing restrictive measures harmful to the performance of the economies of all countries affected.

The propensity to adopt such policies aimed at preventing further loss of reserves is based on a set of beliefs, varying from country to country, which is derived from "rational theories, irrational myths, and the traditional principles or preju- dices," in short, from different values.[2] Machlup suggests that a static emphasis on the size of reserves at a fixed time is wrong. He calls instead for an emphasis on dynamics, i.e., on assured net additions to reserves sufficiently adequate to diminish the need for growth-retarding restrictions on international trade and capital movements. In short, the state of economic knowledge is insuffi- cient to allow a scientific determination of any ideal level of monetary reserves, either for an individual country or for the entire world.

In a later article, Machlup suggests that no one can devise any scientific formula to determine the exact amount by which reserves should increase in any given year:

> This issue is really a political one
> without any possibility of distilling
> an economic theory out of it. If
> governments in most countries are
> composed of staunch free traders,
> they may tolerate substantial defi-
> cits without pushing for higher
> tariffs, lower quotas and stricter
> controls; if governments are com-
> posed of protectionists, national-
> ists and control-lovers, the
> smallest deficits will be pretexts
> for illiberal restrictions. Thus,
> if the "right" amount of reserve
> creation is that which keeps govern-
> ments from adopting new restrictions,
> the managers of the international
> reserve system would have to guess
> where deficits are going to arise
> and would have to gauge the govern-
> ments' marginal propensities to
> restrict and control.[3]

THE POLITICAL DIMENSION OF
INTERNATIONAL MONETARY DECISIONMAKING

Money is a form of power. For the sake of
order, the use of money domestically is controlled
by such national measures as tax and antitrust
legislation. In the world economy, order is obtained principally through a voluntary adherence of
nations to a complex series of institutional and
legal arrangements. These arrangements govern the
conduct of international commerical transactions,
the methods of financing deficits and surpluses in
a country's balance of payments, and the domestic
economic policies which nation-states are expected
to take in response to the development of such
deficits and surpluses.

The smooth operation of the international
monetary system requires a de facto surrender of
national sovereignty. In an age when the latter is
still a valued commodity, there inevitably must be
a major political dimension in what might otherwise
be a "coldly technical discussion of institutional
mechanics." Sovereignty implies different policies,
and with the economic powers of the North Atlantic
each striving to maximize various conflicting value-
rooted ends reflecting their estimations of the
public good, the international monetary reform talks
easily made the transition into the realm of politics.

In certain types of international economic
discussions, a clearcut economic end is involved.
For example, maximum reduction in tariffs on industrial goods has become an end in itself within the
Atlantic community. Industrial trade between certain Atlantic countries (members of the EEC and
member countries of the European Free Trade Association) is already done on a completely tariff-free
basis. On a wider basis, the Kennedy round of
tariff-cutting talks reduced industrial tariffs on
a quid-pro-quo basis throughout the Atlantic community. Protracted talks were also the case here,
but primarily because of the technical problems
inherent in the massive undertaking involved in
cutting tariffs on hundreds of commodities.

Conversely, the disagreement on the control of
liquidity creation introduced a political element

into the monetary reform exercise, the strength of
which was unusual in international economic matters.
Like world politics as a whole, the reform of the
gold-exchange standard was at bottom a pursuit of
value differences. The monetary reform talks, like
politics, evolved less from objective environmental
conditions than from the judgments men made about
those conditions. Similarly, the noted French political scientist, Raymond Aron, characterizes international politics as involving a "constant collision
of wills," since it consists of relations among
sovereign states which claim to govern themselves
independently. It was in fact a collision of value
differences and sovereign wills which lay at the
bottom of the monetary reform exercise.

The contemporary nation-state is not subject
to an external law or to a master arbiter. It is
therefore free to set its behavior in accordance
with the pursuit of various policy ends. The latter
may be psychological, military, or economic in
substance. The whole question of international
monetary reform is an aspect of Atlantic community
politics rather than an esoteric financial problem
to the extent that an equal voice in the control
and use of international liquidity was a means to
achieving European policy ends. The creation of
a new reserve asset was a direct incursion into the
nebulous territory of national sovereignty, a fact
which assured that the monetary reform talks would
be characterized by a clash of national wills and
interests.

Whereas tariff reductions belong to the class
of economic policies that are undertaken mainly for
their own technical merits, the monetary reform
talks belong to the other class of economic policies: those that are undertaken as the "instruments of a political policy--a policy, that is,
whose economic purpose is but the means to the end
of controlling the policies of another nation."[4]

The political elements of international monetary reform are quite subtle, and Machiavellian
power struggles within the talks were conducted
on a most indirect basis. The talks were attended
only by finance ministry and central bank officials
(foreign ministry personnel were absent throughout),
were conducted informally, and used technical, not
diplomatic, language. Ostensibly, the financial

diplomats were seeking an economic answer to an economic problem.

There are no plateaus to balances of power or to foreign policies. They are transitory, ever-changing concepts, and a monetary system developed under the international conditions of the mid-1940's found itself incompatible with the environment of the 1960's. The smooth and successful operation of the gold-exchange standard, with its heavy dependence on the U.S. deficit, was directly related to U.S. hegemony and European acceptance of it.

When both hegemony and acceptance ended, a monetary conflict about power and control developed between the EEC member countries and the United States. Power concerns the significance of the U.S. balance-of-payments deficit as well as the urgency of and responsibility for its elimination. The issue of control concerns first the ability to decide what latitude is to be given to the financing of this and other balance-of-payments deficits and secondly who is to make decisions on the expansion and contraction of international liquidity in general.

Economic analysis and expertise were necessary to evaluate the benefits and drawbacks of the many alternative means of creating a new form of international liquidity. But once out of the exploratory and into the decisionmaking stage, the formerly latent political element of monetary reform materialized and assumed command. This resulted in the fact that the task of the financial diplomats was not simply that of weighing the technical excellence of one plan against another, compromising differences in national viewpoints on technical matters, and then trying to steer the shortest course toward the economically optimal.

The talks had to deal with more complex and divisive controversies such as economic philosophy and domestic politics. The question of altering the gold-exchange standard can also be considered political in the sense that the selection and approval of a reform plan required decisions by a number of national power centers. "Each is concerned with the interest of a narrow constituency as well as with the wider community of interest; each is jealous of its own powers, and cautious

about establishing new precedents that may weaken
its powers."[5] Because of these factors, the talks
in fact were about political means, not economic
ends. They were conducted in a real-world, political environment. This made the shortest path to a
viable policy not a straight line but a circuitous
series of compromises. The least bad rather than
the best or second best, was sometimes all that
could be attained. Private economists had only to
negotiate with their publishers. The financial
diplomats had to negotiate with determined men of
different nationalities who held divergent values.

The economic carrot at the end of the stick
for many more years will be too small for independent
nation-states to abdicate a substantial amount of
sovereignty in the name of economic pragmatism.
Although it has been suggested that "state and war
belong to a pre-economic period of history and are
incompatible with the economic and technical conditions of modern times," the so-called spillover
from economics to politics is still not a meaningful
factor in international relations. The day is still
far removed when, with "the institution of government having been replaced by economic organization,
the problem of universal republic will be solved."[6]

The international monetary reform plan which
emerged after four years was far removed from the
theoretical model of the ideal or even the near
ideal. But the end result of the financial diplomats
cannot be evaluated intrinsically on its own merits.
When, as in this case, the objectives of economic
policies were designed to maximize certain national
values and to increase the power of the nation pursuing them vis-à-vis other nations, then these
policies and their objectives should be weighed in
terms of their enhancement of national power. In
his classic study, Hans Morgenthau observed that an
economic policy which cannot be justified in purely
economic terms might nevertheless be worthwhile in
view of the political policy pursued.[7]

It may be appropriate here to emphasize something observed by a mathematical economist in the
late 1930's: International economic policy is in
the overwhelming majority of cases politics in the
real sense, in that it adopts aims and methods which
are dependent on extraeconomic determinants. The
purpose of trying to justify such policies in

economic terms is usually to hide the inner political intentions which alone can provide a real justi-
fication. "In order not to let the real political
motive become too noticeable, all kinds of embel-
lishments are sought and the specious arguments
which are advanced often give rise to a strange
medley of ideas which could only deceive pedants."[8]

   In the words of another observer, relations
between currencies, like relations between states,
entail problems of strategy. International financial questions must therefore be analyzed as reflections of conflict. It is impractical to think
of these questions in simple terms such as the
requirements of an established social order, inasmuch as those institutional arrangements which do
exist on the international level do not operate as
expressions of an established concensus on the
common good. Since the nation-state is the largest
integrated political community in which such a
consensus can be effectively formulated and enforced, "an analysis of international currency
systems must therefore have as its aim a clarifica-
tion of the balance of power which they reflect, and
of the strategies of dominance and revolt which they
imply."[9]

   Conflicts in the international monetary system
mirror the larger dilemma of world politics as a
whole: the absence of integration and a consensus
of objectives among the sovereign nations of the
world. In the absence of an international or even
Atlantic political community, it is not valid to
transpose the characteristics of the modern state
(with its unified sense of common purpose, single
set of policies and objectives, rational organization of power, and rule of law) to the decentralized
and unharmonious international milieu. This absence
of any systematic political cohesion on a worldwide
basis was responsible for the disruption of the once
smoothly efficient gold-exchange standard. "As with
marriage, the benefits of close international economic relations (a more economical use of limited
resources) can be enjoyed only at the expense of
giving up a certain amount of national independence,
or autonomy, in setting the pursuing economic objectives."[10] Extensive international intercourse
such as that practiced in the Atlantic community
complicates the successful achievement of national
economic objectives in two major ways. First, it

increases the number and magnitude of the disturbances to which each country's balance of payments
is subjected. These imbalances in turn divert
policy attention and instruments of policy to the
restoration of external balances. Secondly, interdependence slows the process by which national
authorities, each acting independently, are able to
attain domestic objectives, e.g., capital inflows
frustrating a deflationary domestic policy.

Such a situation is particularly important
today when the governments of the United States
and Western Europe are more than ever interested in
seeking to achieve a broad range of economic and
social objectives, which includes full employment,
a satisfactory rate of economic growth, reasonable
price stability, an equitable distribution of income, and balanced regional and sectoral development.

The problem of reconciling these domestic
economic objectives with international economic
interdependence is climaxed in a country's balance
of payments--a systematic record of its economic
transactions during a given period of time between
its residents and the residents of the rest of the
world. In seeking to achieve the above mentioned
economic objectives, a country is simultaneously
confronted with the need to avoid prolonged deficits
in its payments imbalances. With supplies of international liquidity--the means by which deficits are
financed--relatively limited, there is a serious
constraint on a country's freedom of action in
seeking to attain its domestic objectives.

The palatable methods available for restoring
balance-of-payments equilibrium are relatively few.
A great many adjustment policies outside the domestic sector, e.g., increases in tariffs, import
quotas, and competitive devaluations have largely
become discredited by international rule and practice. The consequence of this has a greater burden
on deficit (and surplus) countries to restore equilibrium by altering domestic objectives such as
full employment. This is how world trade and the
need to maintain some kind of external equilibrium
come to intrude upon such seemingly domestic economic policies as government expenditures, the manner in which government expenditures are financed,
the level and structure of taxation, and the regula-
tion of business.[11]

The extent to which the monetary system grants flexibility to deficit financing is basically a function of the existence of mutual confidence in the judgment and policies of other countries. Under these circumstances, effective operation of the system presupposes a high degree of political cohesion. The problem of the international monetary system is that an insufficient amount of political cohesion exists in the Atlantic community to assure enough mutual trust to leave a deficit country alone, especially in the face of complex interactions between national economies.

In a system of fixed-exchange rates where adoption of restrictions on the flow of international economic intercourse is frowned upon, there is one major outlet whereby a chronic deficit country can frustrate, at least temporarily, the need to abandon deficit-inducing, expansionary policies: possession of or access to large amounts of the official means of payment, i.e., international liquidity. The larger a country's foreign reserves, the longer it will be able to preserve its autonomy to pursue its chosen economic policy objectives, surplus countries and private currency speculators notwithstanding.

A country's gold- and foreign-exchange reserves are limited to its ability to domestically mine the yellow metal and/or earn liquidity when surpluses in its balance of payments occur. An infinite supply of liquidity for an individual country is therefore theoretically implausible. At this point, it is necessary to introduce the key political-economic variable in the international monetary system: One country has been able to exempt itself from the otherwise universal rule of limited-liquidity holdings. In possessing a national currency which assumed the twin role of international transactions and international reserve currency equivalent in importance to gold, the United States was given extraordinary power. In effect, to autonomously control the major increment to international liquidity was to unilaterally control the course of the monetary system. As a consequence of the worldwide demand for dollars, the United States could pursue domestic and foreign policy objectives with a virtual free hand and without concern for the normal constraints of balance-of-payments discipline. Throughout the early postwar years, Europeans fully acquiesced to the United States having the ability to

create or withhold the bulk of international money.
This was acceptable even though such ability is
nothing short of the power to transmit inflationary
or deflationary conditions to other countries and
the power to influence local conditions of demand
and employment.

International liquidity can, in this light, be
seen to be more than a passive technical tool with
which to finance a balance-of-payments deficit. A
country with sufficient access to it has the ability
to pursue national values and withstand foreign
pressure to abandon policy priorities, unappreciated
by others, which may be contributing to its deficit.
The United States through the late 1950's had unlimited international credit because it could literally "create" liquidity by virtue of the insatiable
European demand for dollars as a reserve and trans-
action vehicle. Yet it would be wrong to ascribe the
extradorinary international financial power of this
country to a Machiavellian policy or ambition.
The dominant role of the United States in the international monetary system was, like its nuclear
preponderance, an unintended consequence of World
War II which so greatly enhanced the nation's power
vis-à-vis the European continent whose power was in
eclipse.

For a period of about fifteen years, more by
virtue of raw economic power than by conscious
design, the United States was able to fulfill a
central concept of power in the international financial sector: the capacity to impose its will upon
other political units. Monetary hegemony also met
Hans Morgenthau's definition of power as including
"the domination of man by man" and comprising "anything that establishes and maintains the control of
man over man." Between 1945 and 1960, this power
relationship was not challenged. The monetary
system worked and worked well as the United States
was allowed to function as the world's central banker
and controller of the system. All continued satisfactorily as long as the surplus countries of
Western Europe were willing or felt compelled to
rely on this country to supply--through foreign aid,
overseas military expenditures, and both short- and
long-term private-capital overflows--the dollars
which provided them both with much needed international buying power and monetary reserves.

A CRITICAL APPRAISAL OF
THE ATLANTIC ALLIANCE

The original need for and later method of reforming the contemporary international monetary system is essentially an aspect of Atlantic community
politics. Reform is in effect an outgrowth of the
conflicting policies between two centers of power in
the free-world economic decisionmaking process, the
United States on the one hand, and the six countries
of the Common Market, Germany, France, Italy, the
Netherlands, Belgium, and Luxembourg on the other.

Atlantic monetary problems, like Atlantic defense problems, have developed as a familiar affair.
Disagreements in both instances concern arrangements
between closely related societies which have been
rendered increasingly obsolete as the postwar balance of power shifts in favor of a rejuvenated
Western Europe and away from a once omnipotent
United States. Atlantic disagreements in the monetary sector thus reflect the same situation as military disagreements in NATO. We have witnessed the
end of that phase of U.S.-European relationships
which was ushered in by the Truman Doctrine and
carried through the Marshall Plan to the construc-
tion of the Atlantic Alliance. Both NATO and the
gold-exchange standard were created at a time of
U.S. hegemony. Both institutions performed remarkably well only so long as the political milieu in
which they were created remained essentially unchanged. The end of European subordination ended
the smooth functioning of each. Henry A. Kissinger
told a Senate Committee in 1966 that it would have
been unprecedented if a policy developed in the late
1940's remained valid for the 1970's, for it is
fallacious to think that the "accident of Europe's
postwar exhaustion" could be perpetuated into a
permanent pattern of international relations. As
President Richard Nixon's National Security Affairs
Adviser later wrote, "Europe's economic recovery
inevitably led to a return to more traditional
political pressures."[12]

The United Stated emerged from World War II
with a strong and relatively stable economy, the
world's largest gold stock, the largest and most

efficient capital market, and an internationally
respected and used currency whose supply was scarce
relative to demand. Since the early 1960's, however, the resulting financial hegemony of the United
States has been consistently dissipated. Aided and
abetted by the persistent inability of this country
to restore equilibrium to its balance of payments,
the surplus countries of Continental Europe, i.e.,
the EEC, have steadily narrowed the gulf of economic
power separating them from the United States. By
their persistent conversions of unwanted dollar
balances into gold, these countries have weakened
the once undisputed strength and acceptability of
the dollar. The greater the diminution of the U.S.
gold stock, the more susceptible was the dollar and
the whole system to a possible collapse. The end
result of this process is to shift international
monetary power toward the reserve-hoarding countries
of Western Europe.

The resurgence of Europe in monetary matters
parallels the nuclear issue. In each case, Europeans have voiced dissatisfaction with a status quo
which originated in the early 1950's at a time when
the United States exerted an unprecedented degree
of unilateral control over the national security
and economic affairs of Western Europe. In NATO,
the United States still retains final control over
whether or not nuclear weapons will be employed in
much the same manner as, until recently, it had
virtually complete control over the essential operations of the gold-exchange standard.

In defense matters, unlike the financial field,
however, the United States can still claim the monopoly on a massive and effective nuclear delivery system. The countries of Western Europe show no signs
of rejecting the idea that the cost would be pro-
hibitive and unnecessary for them to build an independent nuclear arsenal capable of assuring the same
security against Communist encroachments as does the
present United States nuclear "umbrella." This
monopoly notwithstanding, the protected have still
pressed demands of shared control on the protector.

Although the NATO pact, the heart of the
Atlantic Alliance, has endowed the United States with
an extraordinary power over the military fate of its
allies, the treaty was not originally intended to be
either permanent or absolute. Neither was it

inherently supposed to create any kind of union
between Europe and the United States--whether military, political, or economic. Given an original
life of twenty years, NATO's purpose was to give
Western Europe the assurance that the United States
would provide military protection while the former
proceeded with the work of economic recovery which
the latter agreed to support under the Marshall
Plan. There was, however, a tendency for the United
States to equate weakness, dependence, and submis-
siveness with a continued European enthusiasm for
the United States to continue direction of the alliance. U.S. political and military leaders tended
to view Europe as a feuding collection of petty
states which would be more or less indefinitely
reliant on the United States for their survival.
"It came to seem perfectly proper that American
strategists should have sole responsibility for the
way in which Europe would be defended, and that the
political future of Europe should be decided in
Washington."[13] Indeed it was not until some fifteen
years later that U.S. strategic policies were publicly challenged, at first hesitantly, then ever
more explicitly by the Europeans. By then they had
regained sufficient self-confidence that the mere
enunciation of a U.S. policy within the alliance
no longer guaranteed European acquiescence.

     The initiation of an unprecedented experiment
in national economic integration--the European Economic Community--was itself a testament to the
refusal of at least six states to maintain the historical legacy of European bickering and disunity.
Why else should they go through the very trying
process of establishing supranational institutions
to make collective economic policies, seemingly at
the partial expense of their respective sovereignties? Obviously there must be some exceedingly
important and common end which would not be attain-
able without economic union and its inherent sacrifice of national freedom of action. This end is not
logically national security which could be and was
obtained without the price of union by simply maintaining good relations with the United States. To
unite, the countries of Western Europe "have to
desire intensely political fruits which union alone
can bring: real autonomy, power and status."[14]

     NATO's nuclear dilemma developed because of the
inconsistency between the technical requirements of

modern military strategy and the political imperatives of the still sovereign nation-state. Three
factors are primarily responsible for the difficulty: the need for centralized control of military
operations, the desire of each major ally to have
substantial influence on common decisions, and the
political power which control of nuclear weapons is
thought to confer.

It is no coincidence that, if the term "international liquidity" were substituted for the word
"military" in the first item in the above list and
also for the term "nuclear weapons" in the third
item, one would have an excellent, concise explanation of the problems of the international monetary
system.

The United States and Europe remain complemen-
tary but not identical civilizations. Despite the
resurgence of European economic power and the challenge to U.S. hegemony, the United States and
Western Europe will probably continue to be joined
by bonds of friendship, mutual national interests,
and even by some form of military alliance so long
as the Soviet Union poses any kind of threat to the
European Continent. But things will never be the
same as they were in the late 1940's and early
1950's. Although the so-called Americanization of
European commerical activities has produced many
surface similarities, differences still run deeply
between the United States and Europe in culture, in
society, and in personal relations. Although Europe
and the United States are joined by a common heri-
tage and share common cultural values and common
riches in an otherwise impoverished world, they are
not necessarily full political partners. Europe
and the United States might best be considered as
being on parallel rather than identical tracks.
The term "Atlantic community" is essentially a verbal frame of reference to the deeply entrenched
social bonds between the United States and Western
Europe. What must be avoided, however, is to con-
fuse the common values shared by the diverse peoples
who border the Atlantic with a particular form of
political organization between the United States and
Western Europe. "The former is a living reality
based upon three hundred years of shared history;
the latter is a by-product of the cold war."[15]

THE POLITICAL ECONOMICS OF
THE U.S. BALANCE-OF-PAYMENTS DEFICIT

Two of the most sensitive areas of sovereign
power are defense and money: The former determines
a nation's security, and the latter influences its
allocation of material resources. When seen in this
light, it is not coincidental that, given the absence of an over-all political consensus, major
problems confronting the Atlantic community have to
do with the control of nuclear weapons and international liquidity.

As indicated above, the clear-cut U.S. superiority in military technology persists, a fact which
effectively keeps European fingers off the alliance's
nuclear button. But the similarity in the Atlantic
problems ends as soon as the U.S. nuclear stockpile
is compared with its gold stockpile. The former
has grown bigger and better in the 1960's, while the
latter has been decimated. The European offensive
for authority in monetary affairs and the U.S. reaction have understandably reflected the fact that
this country's international economic performance
has not been as successful as its military performance. Nuclear warheads have been produced in greater
quantities than gold bullion.

The decline of U.S. monetary hegemony can be
traced to the deficit in its balance of payments
which (on the liquidity basis) persisted annually,
with only a single exception, from 1950 through 1967.
Within this time span, the United States and Western
Europe exchanged the roles of international creditor
and debtor respectively. This fact alone was sufficient to restore a semblance of equilibrium in
the international balance of monetary power as the
gold-depleted U.S. side of the scale rose, and the
weightier European side, reflecting its accumulation
of gold and dollar assets, descended.

The European reaction to the U.S. balance-of-
payments deficits was not the same after 1957 as
before. With large balances of dollars in their
reserves, balances which continued to grow, the
countries of Western Europe greeted continuing dollar
outflows not with relief as before, but with alarm

and opposition. At this point, the dollar preference of Western Europe was discarded in favor of
a gold preference. This propensity for gold took
the form of obliging the U.S. Treasury Department
to sell gold at $35 an ounce to foreign monetary
authorities (it is the ability to continue to meet
this commitment which is a major factor in maintaining worldwide confidence in the dollar). At
the end of 1968, the U.S. gold supply of $10.9
billion was $12 billion less than it was at the
end of 1957, while, at the same time, total U.S.
short-term foreign liabilities were three times
larger. Most of the lost gold had been transferred
to the accounts of Western European central banks,
all of which bought gold at some time during this
period.

To say that the U.S. balance-of-payments deficit is extraordinary is a classic understatement.
Its causes, severity, duration, method of financing,
impact on other countries, and means of elimination
are all without comparison in international monetary
history. Virtually every other payments deficit in
the world today is the simple result of an excess
of imports over exports. Throughout the period of
the monetary reform exercise, however, the United
States violated this traditional formula by having a
large merchandise-trade surplus (averaging about $4
billion) which was unable to offset governmental expenditures for military and foreign aid purposes,
tourism, and short- and long-term private capital
outflows. Additionally, no other country can claim
to have been able to run up a total deficit of almost $40 billion in only eighteen years or the one
year deficit of $7 billion (measured on the liquid-
ity basis) in 1969. Finally, no other country has
been in a position to finance the overwhelming
proportion of this deficit by the simple holding of
its currency by private and official foreigners in
the form of short-term assets.

The mechanics of the relatively closed-ended
international monetary system are such that one
country's balance-of-payments deficit tends to induce surpluses in other countries. Because of its
persistence and magnitude, the U.S. deficit might
be expected to have "spread the wealth" throughout
a number of countries of the world. This was not
the case. The principal benefactors of the U.S.
gold and dollar drains have been the countries of

Western Europe in general, and the six members of
the Common Market in particular.

However, it is only by using a "strange kind
of politically motivated semantics" that the major
dispenser of equity and portfolio capital can be
labeled as a debtor country. The United States has
been so branded by a narrow and arbitrary system
of balance-of-payments accounting, a system which
cannot look at anything but reserve movements and
changes in short-term foreign liabilities. The importance of increases in long-term income-earning
assets abroad by this country is thus neutralized.
A look at the over-all international balance sheet
of the United States reveals a much stronger picture of health than is generally assumed. Total
U.S. assets and investments abroad at the end of
1968 were in excess of $146 billion, with total lia-
bilities at the $81 billion level. The over-all
net worth of the United States thus amounted to a
robust $65 billion, an amount nearly twice the fig-
ure for 1950. The United States has traded at
least some of its gold to acquire productive, in-
come-producing assets whose value has continued to
increase over the years.

As with everything else about the deficit,
corrective measures are also atypical of conventional textbook remedies. The unique role of the
United States as an exporter of capital has already
been alluded to. In the second place, the relatively low proportion of the U.S. gross national product accounted for by foreign trade means that
deflationary fiscal and monetary measures would
have to be applied with an intolerable intensity
(perhaps six- to eightfold) to obtain a comparable
improvement in the trade balance of European countries, whose foreign trade is a far greater percentage of gross national product. Additionally, the
sheer dollar size of U.S. imports would, if sizably
reduced, lower U.S. exports in reaction to declin-
ing incomes abroad. A third factor in making the
U.S. deficit relatively intractable lies in the
fact that a substantial reduction of federal government expenditures that would clearly reduce the
dollar drain have not been undertaken solely because
of monetary considerations. The foreign-exchange
costs of these expenditures are fixed to the extent
that they support policies deemed as being of overriding importance to national security considerations and the U.S. role in world affairs.

"Donning blinders so as to avoid confronting unpleasant realities is a popular device in international relations." Hence, the thought in the early 1960's that the deficit would not quickly end was "too threatening to the confidence-oriented psychology of most monetary specialists" to be accepted in discussions of the subject.[16] It was comforting to believe, usually quite sincerely, that the U.S. deficit would be attributed to various temporary factors and that it would end once those factors disappeared. Meanwhile, both the discussions and the deficit continued. So too did the absence of any acceptance by the Europeans of the need to extend adjustment discipline to surplus countries.

It is therefore necessary to look beyond simple statistics and into the political realm to assess the full import and impact of the U.S. balance-of-payments deficit. At the heart of the matter is the fact that no matter how deserving or good an international credit risk the United States might be and no matter how unique and useful its balance-of-payments deficit might be as an international financial intermediary, the countries of Western Europe were no longer prepared to willingly extend credit to the United States.

The 1950's were the decade of the dollar. The International Monetary Fund, which had been expected to be the keystone of the gold-exchange standard, performed only a minor role in international finance during these years. Those Western European countries receiving Marshall Plan aid were declared ineligible to draw foreign exchange from the fund, as were most less-developed countries by virtue of their structural-payments imbalances. If it had not been for the generosity of postwar U.S. foreign economic policy, the European return to prosperity would have been substantially delayed. Gratitude and appreciation are not solid grounds for policy in the world of Real-politik, however. While it is possible to make a good mechanical case for a continuing U.S. deficit to provide the countries of Asia, Latin America, and Africa with needed liquidity, any such deficit must rely on its acceptance by this country's principal creditor--Europe.

Neither the United States as the world's central banker nor any commercial bank can indefinitely see its reserves drawn down without eventually being confronted with a financial crisis. A U.S. deficit

coupled with a draw down of its gold stock puts that
deficit squarely within the terms and rules of traditional balance-of-payments discipline. Banks operate only with the consent and the confidence of
their customers, and by the middle of the 1960's,
it had become patently clear that this country was
not going to obtain the consent of its customers,
i.e., its Western European creditors. For economic
as well as political reasons, the Continental European countries remain adamant and united in their
opposition to the U.S. balance-of-payments deficit.

Instinctively, the central bankers of Europe
have become apprehensive at the shrinking ratio of
U.S. gold to its total foreign short-term liabilities. Understandably, they see no intrinsic merit
in either building up limitless balances of dollars
or in extending the United States an infinite level
of credit and patience. It is in the nature of
money that it must be scarce relative to the demand
for it to retain its value. Without doubt, there
is economic logic in opposing what must seem to
the Europeans an open-ended dollar hemorrhage.
The continuing deficit, by eroding confidence in
this country's ability to indefinitely maintain
the present gold value of the dollar, reduced the
attractiveness of the dollar as a reserve currency.
At the same time, it enhanced the attractiveness
of the perennial alternative to paper money--gold.

But caution still does not fully explain why
the Europeans preferred to accumulate inert gold in
lieu of interest-bearing dollar securities (as do
the Japanese, Scandinavians, Canadians, and others)
or to pass up investing their dollars in real economic resources, such as increased imports. In
both cases, relatively high returns in terms of
economic growth could be attained. There was also
a distinct lack of financial rationality in the
European's gold preference to the extent that their
central banks exchanged interest-earning dollars
for inert gold in an amount which exceeded estimations of the likelihood of a dollar devaluation,
i.e., an increase in the monetary price of gold.
A former top Treasury Department official in the
Johnson Administration privately asserted that
foreign central bankers in the early 1960's were
less fearful of an imminent increase in the price
of gold than of domestic criticism for being a party
to the continued embellishment of the superiority

of the dollar. It was not lack of confidence but a
distaste for being viewed as imprudent bankers which
was one of the key factors behind most of Europe's
disinclination to underwrite U.S. deficits and its
position as a world power by providing open-ended
credit. The propensity for an individual European
country to purchase gold was neither a simple barom-
eter of its confidence in the maintenance of the
dollar's gold value nor of the sizes of its balance-
of-payments surpluses. Rather, the propensity was
most rooted in the value attached to enhancing domestic power and influence at the expense of the
United States. The higher this propensity, the more
distasteful it was to continue adding further dollar
balances.

It must also be noted, from an economic point
of view, that there is nothing inevitable or unavoid-
able about persistent Western European balance-of-
payments surpluses. The high priority given to
price stability explains retention of restrictive
fiscal and monetary policies on the European Continent, and this fact has been a major element in
perpetuating these surpluses. This preoccupation
with avoiding inflation notwithstanding, there is
still an economically sound alternative to the balance-of-payments surplus-inducing policies followed
by the Europeans in the early 1960's.

During these years, there was a lagging aggregate demand in the main deficit country, the United
States. Simultaneously, the chief surplus countries
were threatened with inflation. The complimentary
situations of these two groups of countries suggest
a rational and "perfectly elementary" solution.

> All four problems--the output gap in
> the United States, the excess demand
> in Western Europe, the deficit in the
> United States, and the surplus in
> Western Europe--could be reduced or
> elminated if Western Europe, instead
> of accumulating nonearning assets in
> the form of reserves, would reduce its
> restrictions on imports, increase its
> contributions to collective defense,
> or increase its untied aid to under-
> developed countries.[17]

Despite possible political difficulties, there is
no more propitious time, from a domestic point of
view, to reduce import barriers than a time of excess demand, when the public is complaining about
rising prices and producers are enjoying a seller's
market.

Despite the economic benefits of reducing
their chronic surpluses, any move to equilibrium
would have had a political cost to the Europeans:
The United States would have been let off the hook.
The former were not about to dilute their bargaining power and cooperate in halting the trend toward
greater European monetary authority.

From that fateful day in 1960 when spiraling
U.S. short-term foreign liabilities equaled and
then overtook the value of the U.S. gold stock,
the gold-exchange standard assumed an entirely
different complexion. The international monetary
system had then entered a still existent phase in
which its survival had become dependent on the
political willingness of foreign countries, especially in Europe, to hold outstanding and accept new
dollar liabilities as part of their reserves.
Compliance with this unwritten, but all-important
ground rule is difficult, not only because the growing illiquidity of the system's number one debtor
diminished confidence in the dollar, but also because
central banks were being called upon to subsidize a
debtor's policies in which their own governments
would have little or no say, and with which they
might profoundly disagree. In addition to a general
aversion to subsidizing U.S. predominance, its
European creditors also take dim views of certain
alleged consequences of U.S. deficits such as exported inflation, as well as such causes as the war
in Vietnam and the proliferation of U.S. long-term
investments in many of Europe's key industries.
Compounding European unease with the latter item was
the irony that Europe itself was ultimately financing
the unwelcome expansion of the "American Challenge"
by extending long-term credits to the United States
in the form of dollar accumulations.

In an atmosphere where the use of U.S. financial power through the role of the dollar as a reserve currency is being challenged, economic
arguments tend to become pawns in a politician's
game. There can be no doubt that the holding of

dollars was and continues to be a sensitive political issue between the United States and, in varying
degrees, the countries of Western Europe.

NOTES

1. Robert Triffin, "International Monetary
Reform," Economic Bulletin for Latin America, XI
(April, 1966), 11.

2. Fritz Machlup, "The Need for Monetary
Reserves," Banca Nazionale del Lavoro Quarterly
Review, XIX (September, 1966), 200-205.

3. Fritz Machlup, "World Monetary Debate--
Bases for Agreement," The Banker, CXVI (September,
1966), 607.

4. Hans Morgenthau, Politics Among Nations
(New York: Alfred A. Knopf, 1959), p. 28.

5. Robert Z. Aliber, The Future of the Dollar
as an International Currency (New York: Praeger,
1966), p. 133.

6. Hans Morgenthau, Scientific Man Versus
Power Politics (Chicago: University of Chicago
Press, 1946), p. 78.

7. Morgenthau, Politics Among Nations,
op. cit.

8. Oskar Morgenstern, The Limits of Economics
(London: William Hodge and Company, 1937), p. 131.

9. Hans O. Schmitt, "Political Considerations
for International Currency Reform," International
Organization, XXVI (Summer, 1964), 548.

10. Richard N. Cooper, The Economics of Interdependence (New York: McGraw Hill, 1968), p. 4.

11. Ibid., p. 5.

12. Henry A. Kissinger, "Central Issues of
American Foreign Policy," in Kermit Gordon, ed.,

Agenda for the Nation (Washington, D.C.: The
Brookings Institution, 1968), p. 595.

13. Ronald Steel, The End of Alliance (New
York: Delta Books, 1966), p. 30.

14. Harold van B. Cleveland, The Atlantic
Idea and Its European Rivals (New York: McGraw Hill,
1966), p. 139.

15. Ronald Steel, Pax Americana (New York:
Viking Press, 1967), p. 70.

16. Henry G. Aubrey, "Behind the Veil of
International Money," Essays in International
Finance, No. 71 (Princeton: Princeton University
Press, 1969), p. 4.

17. Walter S. Salant, Does the International
Monetary System Need Reform? (Washington, D.C.:
The Brookings Institution, 1964), p. 26.

CHAPTER **2** THE EXPLORATORY
PHASE OF THE
INTERNATIONAL
MONETARY REFORM
TALKS

The expected termination of the U.S. balance-
of-payments deficit and the anticipated growth in
the volume of free world economic intercourse provided the impetus for an official inquiry into previously virgin territory: the possible means of
deliberate creation of international reserves. The
first phase of the monetary reform exercise involved
an academic consideration of the alternative means
of reforming the system conducted by the technicians
of the Group of Ten countries. Still many steps removed from actual negotiations, the period under
consideration was characterized by the effort to
set forth the technical options from which the
policymakers might later select a plan for actual
implementation.

THE ORIGIN OF THE GROUP-OF-TEN STUDIES

By the end of 1961, the ten leading Western
industrial powers recognized that the resources of
the IMF possibly would be inadequate to satisfy the
potential drawing needs of either the United States
or the United Kingdom or to adequately cope with any
sustained weakness in any of the other major currencies. Accordingly, the General Arrangements to
Borrow (GAB) came into effect in October, 1962.
This new arrangement consisted of a commitment by
ten countries--Belgium, Canada, France, Germany,
Italy, Japan, the Netherlands, Sweden, the United
Kingdom, and the United States (Switzerland, which
is not a member of the fund, later associated itself
with the commitment)--to lend a combined total of up
to $6 billion of their currencies to the IMF in cases

where they themselves collectively had determined
such a move was warranted by extraordinary circumstances in the international monetary system.

The GAB had no institutional structure since
it was nothing more than a multilateral lending commitment to the IMF. It was not even utilized for
two years. Thus the birth of the "Group of Ten,"
as the group of countries comprising this special
lending facility was dubbed, was relatively inaus-
picious. Despite its humble beginnings, the group
quickly developed a life and identity of its own,
quite independent of the organization for which it
was designed to serve. It was, above all, the symbol
of the decision by ten countries to retain for themselves the ultimate authority for decisionmaking in
the international monetary field.

The official genesis of the international reform
talks was quietly announced in an obscure press release dated October 2, 1963 and issued by U.S. Treasury Secretary Douglas Dillon "on behalf of" the IMF's
members of the Group of Ten. It described the results of the meeting of the ministers and central
bank governors of those countries, held during the
IMF's annual meeting of that year. The press release
indicated that the participants agreed that eliminating the payments deficits of "some major countries
was the most important objective to be pursued over
the near future," and that the existing national reserves of member countries, supplemented as they were
by the resources of the IMF and by a network of bilateral credit facilities, seemed "fully adequate
in present circumstances" to cope with possible
threats to the stability of the international payments system.

More significant, however, was their decision
to undertake a thorough examination of the outlook
for the operation of the monetary system and of its
probable future needs for liquidity. Such an examination was to be made "with particular emphasis on
the possible magnitude and nature of the future needs
for reserves and for supplementary credit facilities
which may arise."

Accordingly, the deputies of the ministers and
governors were instructed to examine these questions
and to report back on the progress of their studies
and discussions over the course of the coming year.
Although suggesting that they "maintain close working

relations with the IMF and other interested international organizations," the so-called deputies
group was told specifically to submit any of the
suggestions resulting from their studies only to
the ministers and governors of the Group of Ten for
consideration. The meaning of this statement is
clear: The leading economic powers would consider
the liquidity question independently of the IMF or
of any other international body or group of countries.

The first session of the deputies to discuss
the international monetary system convened unceremoniously in Paris on November 5, 1963. Meetings
were held thereafter on the average of two or three
days at a time every month. Participating in the
meetings were the deputies (those second in command
to the finance ministers or central bank governors
of the Group of Ten), plus observers from the
National Bank of Switzerland, the IMF, the Organization for Economic Cooperation and Development (OECD),
and the Bank for International Settlements (BIS).

The immediate historical antecedents to the
initiation of the monetary studies included the relatively old academic cries for reform begun by the
apocalyptical warnings of Robert Triffin in 1959
and the first official suggestion, made in the previous year, that such studies were essential. Since
the end of World War II, Great Britain has had the
over-all weakest balance-of-payments position and
the most speculated-against currency of any country
in the Atlantic community. Understandably, therefore, it was the British Chancellor of Exchequer,
Reginald Maudling, who took the initiative in 1962
and became the first government official to publicly
declare that the time had come to consider structural
changes in the international monetary system.

After alluding to the "universally accepted"
fact that a growing volume of world trade called for
an increase in international liquidity, he went on
to propose the creation of a "mutual currency account" to a somewhat startled IMF annual meeting.
The net effect of such a special account would enable surplus countries to deposit unwanted balances
of reserve currencies (especially pounds sterling)
in the fund and receive a gold-value guarantee to
protect the holder from any loss from devaluation.

Such an arrangement would theoretically provide an
acceptable alternative to the contraction of liquidity resulting from the conversion of unwanted reserve currencies by surplus countries.

The official silence which greeted the so-called
Maudling Initiative reflected the facts that it was
both a premature and unappealing plan. Indeed, it
was opposed or criticized in varying degrees by all
of the other Group of Ten members. Momentum, nevertheless, continued to build for an official study
of possible means of reforming the system. The liquidity dilemma was simply not going to go away. By
1963, all that was required was a public acknowledg-
ment by the economic officials of the Atlantic community that the system might indeed be facing serious
problems and that preparation to cope with them had
to be undertaken while breathing space still existed.

The principal driving force behind the organization of the official talks was U.S. Under Secretary of the Treasury, Robert V. Roosa. His efforts
were in no small way a reaction to his dislike for
some of the more radical reform proposals which were
being aired in unofficial circles. Being of the
suasion that relatively moderate modifications in
existing facilities (as opposed to structural changes)
were the most efficacious means of improving the
monetary system, Roosa determined that the most effective way to assure U.S. influence on the evolution of thought within official circles was to
inaugurate a study group in which he would be an
active participant. Nothing could be gained by
losing the initiative and having some other body,
possibly without adequate U.S. representation, chart
the course of international monetary reform.

A prolonged illness in early 1963 afforded
Roosa an opportunity to think through the entire
monetary situation. He concluded that the time for
action was at hand. Using the hapless Maudling proposal as a starting point, Roosa began sounding out
each of his counterparts in the Group of Ten as to
their views on the usefulness of meeting regularly
for a more searching reanalysis of the existing
system and for a look at where it might be heading.
It was several more months, however, until he became
firmly convinced that the international financial
situation was sufficiently secure--a new U.S. balance-of-payments program had been announced in July--

to minimize the likelihood that the inauguration of
talks would be interpreted as a sign of weakness and
lead to speculative disturbances against the dollar.
Inspired by this U.S. sense of security, the Group
of Ten formally agreed during the annual IMF meeting
in October to initiate liquidity studies.

THE DEPUTIES' REPORT OF 1964

In the part of their talks dealing with the
creation of a radically new international liquidity
mechanism, the deputies focused almost exclusively
on the concept of a Composite Reserve Unit (CRU)
originally suggested by Edward Bernstein, a former
IMF Research Director. CRU's would be instantly
created by the mutual deposit of a specified amount
of each of the Group of Ten's national currencies.
Distributed to each of the participants in proportion to its currency deposit, the CRU's would join
gold and reserve currencies as the principal means
of financing payments deficits. The new units would
be created annually in an amount agreed to by the
participants. The French, backed at this point by
the Dutch, modified this proposal by suggesting the
new units should completely replace dollars (and
pounds sterling) in settling international transactions and that any further accumulations of dollars
by foreign central banks should be barred. Such a
move, in Roosa's view, would actually contract the
world's reserve holdings, and the U.S. delegation
objected to the French and Dutch proposals for posing
an obvious challenge to the special international
role of the dollar and ultimately to the U.S. gold
stock. Neither the Germans nor the Italians took
any firm position at this early time.

In presenting an alternative for the adoption
of the CRU, the United States continued to stress
the adoption of reciprocal currency holdings and the
further expansion of the credit facilities which had
been set up to meet short-term liquidity problems.
Roosa's unwavering allegiance to the gradual approach
was clearly voiced in his May, 1964, address to the
American Bankers Association. After conceding that
new forms of liquidity would emerge as needs changed,
he declared that he wished to place emphasis not on
the specific instruments themselves but on the
process that would create them--the process of

evolutionary change shaped by common appraisal and
cooperative action.

In mid-June, 1964, a meeting of ministers and
governors of the Group of Ten reached a number of
decisions concerning the future course and substance of the deputies' study. The basic step forward was the agreement in principal to advocate an
increase in quotas at the IMF meeting scheduled for
September. Secondly, it was agreed that a summary
report of the deputies' liquidity study would be
published, together with a ministerial statement,
in late July or early August. In this way, it
would be timed to coincide with the release of the
IMF's own liquidity study scheduled to be included
in its annual report. It was further decided to
continue studying the longer-term issues of world
liquidity problems after the publication of their
report.

By the end of June, therefore, the general
framework of the initial deputies' report had been
established. All that remained was to have a final
draft drawn up by the five-man secretariat and approved by the deputies themselves. Because of their
many responsibilities above and beyond the liquidity
study, most of the actual drafting of this report
was done by the secretariat. They were, in effect,
deputies to the deputies of the U.S. Treasury representative and of the representatives of the
French, German, British, and Dutch central banks.
It was those men who were charged with the frequent-
ly complex and perplexing task of adopting language
acceptable to all of the major participants.

According to one of the U.S. participants in
the deputies' deliberations, the modest outcome of
this first study had become evident as early as the
fifth meeting, held in Washington, D.C. in April.
Shortly after that meeting, the press was already
correctly predicting that all that was likely to
emerge from the two official liquidity studies
would be a minor increase in fund quotas, with backing for new forms of international liquidity still
in highly conservative form, still described on highly guarded terms, and with major decisions still
complacently postponed.

Behind this prognostication was the increasingly obvious fact that the consensus necessary to

recommend adoption of any type of truly radical
method of monetary reform was totally and hopelessly
absent at that time among the deputies. Roosa's
assessment of late 1963 was still valid: The wide
divergence in fundamental views on reform held in
the Group of Ten meant that no important forward
progress in the evolution of the system could occur
until the major participants had come closer to some
common framework of analysis.

The deputies' report of 1964 was a compromise
document, couched in least common denominator
language, which openly referred to the existence
of a number of divergent views. As the report itself admitted, "given the complexity of the problem
referred to us, it is not surprising that a number
of views were expressed as to the areas which most
deserve further study or action for the longer run
improvement and strengthening of the international
monetary system."[1]

The report noted that some of the deputies believed that the present monetary system implied at
least a partial reliance on the continued accumulation of reserve currency holdings, and therefore
wished to stress the disadvantages of dependence for
the creation of new reserves on the balance-of-payments deficit of a reserve-currency country. Other,
less disenchanted, deputies stressed the primary
desirability of simply building on the accomplish-
ments and flexibility of the existing gold-exchange
standard. It was their view that "principal reliance should be placed on strengthening the international credit component of the present system, and
on the increase in reserve assets created when official credits are extended either through the fund
or in some other form."[2]

Perhaps the most interesting and significant
outgrowth of this initial monetary study was the
embryonic emergence of the policy positions which
later set the tone and course of the international
monetary reform negotiations. France and the United
States immediately found themselves with dissimilar
outlooks. The former had opted for the introduction
of a new reserve asset which would be created "according to appraised over-all needs for reserves."
The latter had opted for the simple extension of
claims on the IMF, the volume of which could "be
enlarged to meet an open need." Lying in between

these divergent policies was the German-Italian
proposal of a possible "harmonization" ratio for
the gold and foreign exchange composition of national reserves.

To summarize, the initial deputies' report of
1964 recommended little in the way of innovation
and changed nothing. The U.S. emphasis on existing facilities was opposed by the Europeans, who
could not be talked out of their demand for future
study within the Group of Ten of the possibility of
creating a new international reserve asset.

Simultaneous with the August publication of
the deputies' report was the release of the IMF's
1964 annual report, which contained the results of
the fund's first study of international liquidity
since completion of an informal survey in 1958.
Like the deputies' report, the IMF study was unsen-
sational and devoid of any major recommendations
for further action. It too agreed that the over-all
level of liquidity was adequate for the time being,
and that international credit arrangements had
proved useful. Likewise, it warned that on the one
hand there was likely to be a persistent and substantial growth in the demand for international
liquidity, while, on the other, the sources of reserve growth during the past decade seemed likely
to provide a smaller annual rate of increase over
the decade to come.

After a lengthy review of the fund's role as a
source of reserves, the report listed several methods
by which the IMF "might enhance its contribution to
the supply of international liquidity of a more or
less unconditional kind." Among those methods suggested was making members' access to some portion of
the credit tranches (those above the virtually automatic first, or gold, tranche) more automatic or "to
substitute for a portion of the gold subscription to
the fund an alternative method of payment." Thus,
a country could have an increase in guaranteed drawing rights without a payment to the IMF of gold or
foreign exchange. Also suggested was an arrangement
in which the fund could purchase special assets, such
as bonds, from its members in exchange for alloting
them some form of increased drawing rights. This
procedure would put the fund in the "investment"
business.

THE REPORT OF THE STUDY GROUP ON THE
CREATION OF RESERVE ASSETS

Prior to the finalization of their report, the
deputies and ministers had become aware of the fact
that it would be necessary to initiate a followup
study. Such a study would be given the responsibility of developing the various types of proposals
for the creation of reserve assets which the deputies had not been able to study in detail. Accordingly, creation of the Study Group on the Creation
of Reserve Assets had been formally sanctioned in
the deputies' report. The group's chairman, Rinaldo
Ossola of Italy, described it as being designed to
bring out the similarities and differences of the
underlying principles, functions, and modes of operation of these proposals. In addition, the study
group was to report on the "economic and financial
repercussions" of the various proposals on the reform of the international monetary system. In
effect, the group was supposed to assemble the elements necessary to enable first the deputies and
then the finance ministers and central bank governors
to evaluate the merits of the individual proposals.
But it was to do this without "expressing preferences, making recommendations or seeking points of
agreement for a solution of the different problems."[3]

The study group consisted of twenty-five senior
economic officials who were generally one rank below that of the deputies. They were joined by eight
"participants" from three international organizations
(IMF, OECD, and BIS). As requested by the ministerial meeting of the Group of Ten held in December,
1964, the report of the study group was presented to
the deputies on May 31, 1965. The 113-page study
was made public three months later. That the report
was to be a factual, technical study of many reform
proposals was emphasized in its introduction, which
stressed that the group had been "mindful that our
instructions were not to express preferences among
individual proposals." In short, the report was designed to present objectively a list of practical
alternatives, not to offer a consensus.

The Ossola report was essentially an exhaustive
amplification of reform proposals only briefly alluded
to in the deputies' report of 1964. It introduced

nothing really new to the international monetary reform exercise. Yet, it did keep momentum for reform
alive and did climax the academic or exploratory
phase of the talks. Hence, the report's only real
significance was that, for the first time, it provided a systematic and in-depth analysis of the
technical mechanics of the various officially spon-
sored plans to create a new international reserve
asset. In making no pretense of attempting to arrive at a consensus, the report accomplished its
original objective, i.e., examining the technical
issues in detail. It no doubt assisted later deliberations by crystallizing and spotlighting the divergent opinions on the four fundamental issues:
the link between gold and the new reserve asset,
the width of membership in the plan, the role of
the IMF, and the rules for decisionmaking in the
reserve-creation process.

Perhaps the most striking thing about the so-
called Ossola report, however, is how quickly its
contents were overtaken by events and made obsolete.
Three months before the finalization of the report,
President de Gaulle in effect had swept aside the
French CRU proposal with a demand for the return to
the old gold standard. Both the CRU proposal and
its chief advocate, French Finance Minister Giscard
d'Estaing, were lame ducks by the time the report
was finally published. By early 1966, the French,
for reasons to be discussed in the next chapter,
would disavow the CRU or any other new reserve asset.

Also destined to be discarded were the British
proposals for the provision of an alternative reserve asset to holders of reserve currencies.

Conspicuous by its absence was any clear-cut
U.S. persuasion or sense of direction. The reason
for this lay in the fact that most of the Ossola
report was written at a time of transition in the
U.S. Treasury Department. Secretary Dillon had
left in early April, 1965, and Under Secretary Roosa
had resigned at the end of 1964. Consequently, U.S.
strategy and policy during the preparation of the
Ossola report were first and foremost a holding action. U.S. tactics were simply designed to discourage anything from firmly gelling until the vital
but vacant top leadership posts in the Treasury Department were filled.

U.S. suggestions were therefore limited to a
continued emphasis on the evolutionary process,
specifically through more liberal drawing arrangements in the IMF. The U.S. delegation did display
a vehement negativism in its continued opposition
to the French CRU proposal, which, with its direct
link with gold, threatened to replace the dollar as
a reserve instrument. The U.S. delegates derided
the CRU as being merely a disguised form of increasing the price of gold and a kind of "trading stamp"
for gold holders.

With both the Italians and Germans joining the
United States in presenting no formal national plan
for reserve creation in the Ossola report, the document could not provide a lasting record of country
preferences. Since the one comprehensive national
plan it did contain was soon discarded, the real
carryover effects on the later stages of the liquidity negotiations may be considered as nominal.

NOTES

1. "Statement by Ministers of the Group of Ten
and Annex Prepared by Their Deputies" (London: Her
Majesty's Stationery Office, 1964), p. 9.

2. Ibid.

3. Rinaldo Ossola, "On the Creation of New
Reserve Assets: The Report of the Study Group of
Ten," Banca Nazionale del Lavoro Quarterly Review,
XVIII (September, 1965), p. 273.

3

POLITICALIZATION
OF THE
INTERNATIONAL
MONETARY REFORM
TALKS

The need to reform the international monetary system had been conceived by the refusal of the surplus countries of Europe to finance the continuing U.S. balance-of-payment deficit. Now, having spent their infancy in a period of exploratory studies, the monetary reform talks would "come of age" with the blossoming of traditional interstate political maneuvering. This chapter investigates the politicalization process from the standpoint of varying national interests producing equally varying national policies on monetary reform.

NATIONAL INTERESTS AND LIQUIDITY
POLICIES OF THE UNITED STATES AND FRANCE

As intangible and difficult to explain as sovereignty, the concept of national interests has been described as the general, long-term, and continuing purpose which government officials see themselves and their state as serving. In dictating the nature of a state's long-term foreign-policy efforts and governing what it does in a short-term context, the concept of national interest gives policy a general orientation toward the external environment and serves as the controlling criterion of decisionmaking in immediate circumstances.[1]

There is an immense schism between General de Gaulle's vision of an independent Europe amenable to French leadership and fully equal to the United States on the one hand, and U.S. conceptions of its permanent leadership role in the world and its alliance with a united but compliant Western Europe on

the other hand. In between these somewhat irreconcilable senses of purpose, i.e., sets of national
interests, were Gaullist France's partners in the
EEC, Germany, Italy, the Netherlands, Belgium, and
Luxembourg (who is not a member of the Group of Ten)
--the "Five." These countries either lack the sta-
ture and ambitions of a major power or have a special
military dependence on the United States. However,
the Five, like France, have been blessed with a
swift economic recovery from World War II and therefore share a certain taste for ending their tutelage
under U.S. hegemony, vintage 1945-55. What results
is a situation where these countries have one leg
of their foreign policy oriented toward gradual
European autonomy and the other leg oriented toward
an Atlantic approach embracing continued cooperation
with the United States.

Three different but connected sets of national
interests were thus functioning in the Atlantic community during the liquidity talks. This situation
manifested itself both in the clash of French and
U.S. policies and the straddling of the two extremes
of the international monetary reform spectrum by
the Five. They agreed in substance with the French
drive to end U.S. monetary hegemony and subject the
United States to traditonal balance-of-payments
discipline, but simultaneously they approved of the
United States drive to negotiate a mutually satisfactory and economically rational reform agreement
well in advance of the liquidity shortage expected
to eventually result from a U.S.-payments equilibrium.

In the absence of any absolutely acceptable and
perfect technical criterion for determining the quantitative needs of the world for international liquidity, it is to be expected that subjective national
interests would be instrumental in shaping each of
the members of the Group of Ten in their basic approaches to this politically sensitive subject. An
understanding of the evolving national policies during the talks presupposes an understanding of national attitudes with regard to such fundamental issues
as the need for balance-of-payments discipline and
the need for increased international liquidity--and
the reasons behind these attitudes.

The United States enjoys both the benefits
and the vulnerabilities of possessing the world's
principal reserve currency. It is Keynesian-oriented,

in that national economic policies emphasize full
employment and growth rather than price stability and
balance-of-payments equilibrium. Because of its propensity to incur balance-of-payments deficits, the
United States would benefit from relatively large increases in international liquidity--as supplements
rather than substitutes for dollars. Since these
traits are all shared to some extent by Great Britain,
the Anglo-Saxons might be viewed as monetary bed-
fellows.

On the other hand, the continental countries
remain fearful of inflation, have all at one point
enjoyed persistent payments surpluses and an abun-
dance of monetary reserves in the 1960's, and are
opposed to the perpetual financing of the U.S. (and
British) deficit. Throughout the mid-1960's, these
countries discounted the probability of any imminent
liquidity shortage and the need to reflate their almost too stable economies. Instead, they stressed
the haphazardness, inequity, and vulnerability of a
system in which the bulk of reserve increments is
heavily dependent on the unpredictable size of U.S.
payments deficits and on the precarious willingness
of foreign central banks to finance them by continuing to extend credit to the United States.

Two relatively clear-cut sets of national interests exist with regard to the questions of the
speed of balance-of-payments adjustment and the volume at which new international liquidity is to be
created. One set of interests is applicable to the
international debtors--the United States and the
United Kingdom--who view deflationary measures as
anathema. The other set is attributable to the international creditors who are convinced that a lack
of economic discipline on the part of the Anglo-
Saxons has created an inflationary surplus of liquidity. They feel that only a tight rein on the
availability of liquidity will bring sufficient pressure for adjustment to bear on the monetarily and
fiscally irresponsible policies of the reserve-currency countries.

The bases of these conflicting positions in the
monetary debate lie in a gray area bordered on by
economics proper, economic philosophy, politics, and
even psychology. The quantity of liquidity which
might be available is inextricably linked with the
speed of adjustment in deficit countries. Yet the
concept of adjustment, no matter how interesting

theoretically, is controversial mainly in relation
to sterling and the dollar: "It involves the
strength of two major reserve currencies and their
future role in the network of international finance.
This is a highly political matter quite apart from
the formidable technical problems."[2]

Postwar U.S. international monetary policy
has been designed to promote a sense of cooperation
in which all countries can pursue full employment,
price stability, and rising living standards by
means of economic growth and the fewest possible
constraints on the free flow of international trade
and capital. Maximum trade with a minimum of obstacles requires a healthy supply of liquidity. It was
for this basic reason that in the post-payments deficit era, the United States wanted to discount the
eventuality of a liquidity crunch forcing free-world
countries to adopt defensive beggar-thy-neighbor
measures which inhibit both domestic economic growth
and international economic intercourse. "Dynamic
growth in a dynamic world economy"--for its own sake
and as a reaction to the challenge of Communism--be-
came a major objective of U.S. foreign economic
policy. Its attainment, according to former Treasury Secretary Henry Fowler, means "growing international trade, growing domestic supplies of money,
growing national outputs, and growing real incomes
and profits." The United States feared that unless
monetary reserves grew at least in proportion to
the more severe payments imbalances accompanying
larger trade and greater financial interdependency
among nations, the dramatic postwar growth of world
trade and international economic specialization
risked curtailment.

U.S. policy in this area has always had to
carry water on both shoulders. Its genuine desire
to assure maximum flexibility in financing balance-
of-payments deficits has been tempered, especially
in the 1961-64 period, by the equally important objective of preserving the role of the dollar as the
leading international reserve and transactions
(vehicle) currency. The opposition to any new reserve asset which might pose a clear and present
danger to the dollar's role is based on the simple
calculation that it is in the U.S. national interest
to preserve the dollar's reserve currency and trans-
actions-vehicle functions.

Although not without burdens (e.g., the virtual elimination of devaluation as a viable means of restoring equilibrium), ownership of the world's key currency has been very profitable to the United States. In any description of these advantages, exhibits one and two would have to be short-term liabilities (in late 1969) of $28 billion to private foreign dollar holders and the $12 billion liability to official dollar holders, i.e., foreign central banks. Each of these categories is derived from this country's spending far more abroad than it earns. The holding of dollar assets by foreigners has enabled the United States to contract quasi-permanent credit in excess of $40 billion. Such indebtedness is unheard of in other countries, for this financing is inextricably linked to the unique international role of U.S. currency. Given the limited size of its gold stock, it enabled the United States to pursue domestic and foreign policies which it could not afford in the absence of the special role of the dollar.

Former Treasury Under Secretary for Monetary Affairs, Robert V. Roosa, affirmed to a Congressional Subcommittee in 1962 that this country derives both long-term advantages (earnings from investments and loans) and short-term advantages (credit which can be obtained for relatively longer periods and in relatively larger amounts available to any other country) from being banker to the world. The credit standing of a banking center is such, he said, that "it can, in effect, borrow to meet its needs in almost an imperceptible fashion, without the necessity of arranging and negotiating loans as other borrowers must do." Roosa, as chief architect of U.S. international monetary policy in the 1961-64 period, has written that it is important to weigh heavily "the positive consequences for the prestige and influence of the United States throughout the world that arise from the thousands of individual relationships necessarily created in the day-to-day uses that are made of dollar facilities by traders and bankers and governments in so many other countries." In the long run, he felt that this country would surely be able to earn benefits and to enjoy privileges that would more than offset the strains or burdens associated with the responsibilities of maintaining the world's primary vehicle and reserve currency.[3]

The two cornerstones of the U.S. Government's policy toward its balance-of-payments deficit were, first, that its end was dictated by the larger need for international monetary stability, and secondly, that it would and could be eliminated in short course, without any serious domestic and worldwide disruption. Francis M. Bator, a White House adviser specializing in international economic affairs in the Johnson Administration, has argued that, in the absence of any really dependable central bank cooperations, a large and persistent U.S. payments deficit "would risk, with increasing probability over time, heavy private and small-central-bank gold speculation, growing nervousness among the big dollar-holding central banks, and continuing exposure to a bear raid on the dollar which would force the U.S. to close up shop in New York and to renegotiate the international money rules in a setting of crisis."[4]

The United States was determined to eliminate its balance-of-payments deficit, but at the same time, it was going to do this only within predetermined limits. This basic U.S. attitude as to how it would go about eliminating the deficit was outlined in a 1965 statement before Congress by the then Treasury Secretary, Douglas Dillon. From the start, the government had sought to attain equilibrium within the "framework of a more vigorous domestic economy, operating closer to its full potential and offering improved incentives for investment." He said the beginning of the Kennedy Administration was a time of excessive unemployment, underutilized manufacturing capacity, and an insignificant rate of economic growth, all of which needed prompt correction. The traditional deflationary tonic for deficits was clearly unacceptable.

In effect, the Secretary indicated, economic stagnation was the principal concern to the new Administration. Acceleration, not braking, was called for. Hence, it was deemed essential to spur more rapid growth at home, while finding the solution to external problems in the rising productivity and improved climate for domestic investment that this growth would induce. Dillon added that the United States had a new and unique kind of balance-of-payments problem. "Because the standard remedies were inapplicable, a new course had to be charted."

Speaking before the IMF's 1965 annual meeting
in Washington, D.C., former President Lyndon B.
Johnson recognized that it was no longer "appropriate or possible" for one country alone to provide,
through its deficits, the major source of new world
reserves. This belief led the United States to take
"firm action" to end the dollar outflow and to accept the need to undertake whatever future action
was necessary. President Johnson added that it was
both in the interests of the United States and in
the interests of those who rely on the dollar as a
reserve currency to maintain balance of payments in
equilibrium. "The world not only expects but the
world requires that the dollar be as good as gold."

Treasury Secretary Henry H. Fowler had analyzed
the official U.S. determination to restore equilibrium in more technical detail, in a speech made
in July of that year:

> It is imperative not simply to reach
> balance in our payments for a quarter
> or two, or even for a year, but to
> sustain equilibrium over time. The
> reasons are clear. Our fourteen years
> of deficits have resulted in a large
> outflow of dollars to the rest of the
> world. Because there is worldwide
> confidence in the stability of those
> dollars and because they are converti-
> ble into gold at the fixed price of
> $35 an ounce, those dollars are widely
> used to finance international trans-
> actions, and other countries hold them
> alongside gold in their official re-
> serves. . . .
>
> If we allowed our deficits to con-
> tinue, or if we lapsed back into pro-
> longed deficit after a brief period of
> surplus, we would undermine world con-
> fidence in the dollar and impair its
> usefulness as a world reserve and
> leading currency. Dollars would
> return to our shores as claims on our
> gold, thus depleting instead of supple-
> menting world financial resources.5

If balance-of-payments adjustment is one major
aspect of the international monetary problem, then

the question of the availability of international liquidity is a second. In a sense, they are recipro-cal of each other; the amount of liquidity available to a deficit country is a big determinant of the speed and severity of adjustment policies adopted. At the heart of the Roosa-designed U.S. plan for the provision of adequate liquidity were various credit arrangements, which, together with some other refinements, could, within the existing system, generate sufficient reserves to meet the world's growing liquidity needs for the foreseeable future.

The creation of any new reserve unit, such as the CRU, was deemed unnecessary by the chief mone-tary policymakers in the Kennedy Administration. They believed increments of new liquidity fully consonant with the growing needs of the global econo-my could most efficiently be assured simply from the expansion of the already existing ad hoc credit fa-cilities, most of which were devised by Roosa and his associates to ameliorate the disruptive effects of the U.S. deficit. Additionally, Roosa would suggest that a system of multiple reserve currencies could be established as an additional source of re-serves.

In 1962, Roosa dismissed the Triffin-inspired concept of a world central bank on the grounds that any elaboration of the idea would be a "fruitless exercise" since the basic premises on which the es-tablishment of such a superbank rests were unsupport-able. The fatal shortcoming of such a bank would be its issuance of the "most high-powered" money ever generated by a manmade institution, which nonethe-less would have no supporting supergovernment to guarantee its debts or claims. He argued that such a bank would have far weaker resources than the United States, and yet the performance of the world's richest country had itself repeatedly been chal-lenged. "Simple to establish the superbank would re-quire all countries of the world to give up their present reserves and accept instead the fiat issue of a superauthority existing without a superstate. But assuming that could be done, what would happen when differences of view begin to exercise conflict-ing pulls upon the central organization?"[6]

Starting from the basic assumptions that the price of gold at $35 an ounce was immutable and that "a solution of the balance-of-payments deficit is

fundamental," the U.S. approach foresaw the time
that a U.S.-payments surplus, often feared as having
the effect of shrinking international liquidity,
would be financed by building up holdings of other
currencies that were not thought of as reserve
currencies. Such a currency pool would not only
prevent any possible liquidity squeeze, but it would
also provide a means of handling the bulk of short-
term deficit swings in the U.S.-payments position.
This would leave gold reserves available to cover
more fundamental adjustments. The net effect of this
latter proposal, Roosa explained, would be to multi-
lateralize the system of national reserve currencies
"within a framework that would place great stress on
still further cooperation among monetary authorities
of the type that has been so successfully developed
over the past year or so."

The former Treasury Under Secretary was completely confident that the existing system was fully
capable of providing the steady growth of monetary
reserves needed to serve the trade requirements of
an expanding world. After all, in addition to the
new credit arrangements (the GAB, swaps, and so
forth), there was still the strength of the dollar
to anchor the system:

> Dollars are still the currency to
> which all countries turn for a sub-
> stantial part, if not the entire
> amount, of their international pay-
> ments. Our financial institutions
> and our markets are increasingly
> well equipped to service the payments
> requirements of the world. It is a
> role which naturally accompanies our
> leading economic and political posi-
> tion. The only reason that the use-
> fulness of the dollar has come into
> doubt is that, for some time, dollars
> have been added to the "money supply,"
> i.e., the monetary reserves of other
> countries at too fast a pace.[7]

A system of reciprocal holdings of national
currencies would create new monetary reserves to the
extent that a key-currency country would not expend
its reserves to finance a payments deficit. Instead,
it would increase its short-term liabilities to the
surplus country accumulating balances of its currency.

In effect, the former would be borrowing from the
latter. What Roosa was proposing was actually nothing unique--this is precisely the method by which
the U.S.-payments deficit has always created international liquidity. The multiple reserve or multiple key-currency approach would simply expand the
procedure to include other currencies as insurance
against a U.S.-payments surplus producing a world
liquidity squeeze.

Both Roosa's initial abhorrence of a new international reserve unit and any increase in the price
of gold through a devaluation of the dollar reflected
his visceral determination to preserve the essence
of the gold-exchange standard: the paramount role
of the dollar as a reserve and transactions currency.
This was the overriding value which guided the course
of his international monetary policies. His emphasis
on "assuring the free world's liquidity" in a post-
U.S. deficit era is testimony to the fact that there
was nothing incompatible with the U.S. preference
for retention of the monetary status quo with its
twin objective of assuring that no shortage of liquidity would ever hamper the growth of international
economic intercourse.

The United States privately acknowledged the
need to discuss possible changes in the international monetary system with its Group-of-Ten partners
well before October, 1963. But in the best tradition of power politics, it wanted to wait until it
could negotiate from a position of maximum strength.
Public insistence by the United States until late
1963 that a full-scale study of the system was unnecessary and premature was itself dictated by the
imperatives of Administration-interpreted national
interest. The U.S. Government had to oppose such
suggestions until the strength of the dollar was
clearly reestablished. The world's financial markets
were in such a nervous state, Roosa felt, that even
a slight hint of support for radical change at that
time "could have destroyed confidence in the existing payments arrangements and jeopardized any prospects for orderly progress toward eventual major
reforms." And there would have been suspicion that
the United States, if it then persisted in advocating major currency reforms, was really seeking
relief from its own immediate balance-of-payments
pressures.[8]

The U.S. dollar had the most to lose from any sudden and major upheaval in the international monetary status quo. Hence, this country adapted a "go-slow" attitude during the first eighteen months of the monetary reform talks. There was a mutual harmony between this approach and Roosa's sincerely held belief that it was essential to develop "friendly, harmonious working relations" as a precondition for any successful introduction of a more advanced form of financial cooperation. By temporarily working within the relatively less radical framework of swaps and multiple reserve currencies, he felt the Group of Ten could share in an opportunity to test out some of the "building blocks" for what could eventually be a major reform effort. In short, more experience was necessary in the new field of multilateral monetary responsibility before a base for a sustainable reform could be established.

American international monetary policy from 1961 through 1964 remained fixed on the need for preventing any spontaneous combustion or gathering momentum that could in any way have led to a negation of the paramount role of the dollar. The main U.S. objective was to assure that any potential changes in the system which might be seriously discussed could "coexist" with existing arrangements. Roosa wanted to preserve the advantages to the dollar of serving as a vehicle currency, and he thought that this required the maintenance of the dollar's reserve-asset role, at least on the scale that had been reached up to that time. Continuation of the transactions function of the dollar was thus dependent on continuation of its reserve function, a desired end in itself.

The efforts of the United States to preserve and protect the role of the dollar were in no small way related to the nation's distrust of the CRU as introduced by the French during the initial deputies' study of 1963-64. As one official explained it, there was alarm on the part of the U.S. Government that in pressing for a full-scale study of the gold-exchange standard, the French were actively seeking a means to knock out the role of the dollar as an international reserve. It was feared at this time that a new, artificial unit would both supplement and supplant the dollar as the major reserve unit.

The two most important concerns of French foreign policy under former President de Gaulle were the insurance of French independence of action and the cultivation of France's role as a leading world power. He apparently deemed attainment of either role as being inconsistent with French cooperation in a U.S.-dominated military alliance or in a dollar-dominated monetary system. The country's pursuit of its national interests inexorably brought it into conflict with the policies and interests of the United States, particularly because a primordial fact of Gaullist foreign policy was its insistence that the United States was far too powerful, and, regardless of its intentions, could not keep from trying to dominate the affairs of other nations. De Gaulle's abhorrence of U.S. hegemony and power meant that achievement of the independence and world-leadership role for France, which he so craved, presupposed restoration of some semblance of a balance of power in the Atlantic community in particular and in the world in general. His anti-U.S. thrusts were therefore not vicious ends in themselves but unemotional means to attain French values in an all too Americanized world.

The dollar is the economic symbol of U.S. power. French international monetary policy therefore was logically the antithesis of U. S. policy: It sought the prompt removal of the dollar from what was deemed its inordinate, unnecessary, unfair, and ill-advised position of privilege and power. The gold-exchange standard had permitted the United States to pursue political, economic, and military policies with virtually no regard to their balance-of-payments cost. Seemingly limitless and automatic credit extensions offered by dollar-hungry foreigners had created a system clearly intolerable to the General. The elimination of the gold-exchange standard represented for de Gaulle the emancipation of the nonreserve currencies from the dollar, the liberation of the international currency system from the direct influence of U.S. controls, the potential creation of some direct influence on the U.S. balance-of-payments policy, and the containment of further U.S. foreign investments.

Monetary autonomy had become an aspect of the larger French value of political autonomy. The credit worthiness of the dollar was attacked by de

Gaulle in a policy not unrelated to his attack on
the credibility of the U.S. nuclear guarantee. The
objective in both cases was more political than
functional: "to reduce American prestige and influence in Europe in the interest of France's freedom of action and his own design for Europe."9

The official halt to French monetary cooperation with the United States was heralded in a press
conference held by President de Gaulle on February
4, 1965. According to the General, the fact that
other states in principle had accepted dollars on
the same basis as gold had tended to neutralize the
U.S. payments deficit. This in turn enabled the
United States to indebt itself abroad at no cost.
What this country owned abroad, "it pays for, at
least partially, with dollars which it alone can
issue, instead of paying entirely with gold, which
has a real value, which must be earned to be possessed, and which cannot be transferred to others
without risks and sacrifices." De Gaulle reasoned
that the net result of this situation was to make
the gold-exchange standard not so much an international system as a means of credit belonging to
one country.

The French further imparted their argument that
the gold-exchange standard "was no more" to the assembled economic dignitaries at the 1966 IMF annual
meeting. Owing to the privileged position reached
by certain reserve currencies, the system was no
longer working according to its definition, claimed
the French Finance Minister, Michel Debre. He argued
that the conversion of surplus dollars into gold was
considered "by some curious mental aberration, as a
dangerous, indeed as an inadmissable action, whereas
this is one of the principles of the gold-exchange
standard in its normal functioning. Conversions
into gold have the advantage of ensuring that unlimited credit is not granted to deficit countries."

Prior to de Gaulle's taking an active interest
in the question of international monetary reform,
the French, through Finance Minister Valery Giscard
d'Estaing, had sought the same dilution of the power
and prestige of the dollar. But his means to this
goal was through the introduction of a new international reserve unit. The French-sponsored CRU
was designed as a technical and indirect displace-
ment of the dollar's role as the partner to gold in

monetary reserves. France thus became the first
country to officially support creation of a new reserve asset. As early as the 1963 fund meeting,
Giscard suggested that the cessation of the U.S.-
payments deficit should immediately be followed by
a thorough examination of the international monetary
system, particularly on the assumption that the development of world trade might require increasing
liquidity. He stated: "If such should be the case,
we should also make our judgment on the nature of
the liquidity and on the methods used for providing
it."

At the next IMF gathering, one year later, the
gold base and bias of the French Finance Minister's
reform plan was becoming more readily apparent. It
was argued that the importance of gold to the monetary system was not due to any "charm inherent in
the metal itself," but rather to the fact that with
separate national sovereignties throughout the world
acting freely in the monetary field, without recourse to arbitration, and not subject to coercion,
attention would have to be focused on gold, "the
only monetary element outside the scope of government action."

Giscard did qualify France's preoccupation with
the central role of gold by admitting doubts that
the pace at which it was mined would spontaneously
adjust its volume to the needs of the world. For
this reason, France foresaw the eventuality of having to seek out "supplementary sources for supplying
owned reserves." Were the need for additional liquidity in fact to materialize, there should be a "con-
certed and limited recourse to additional fiduciary
means. . . . Such a substitution should be brought
about gradually and not by disrupting the present
system."

In the latter part of 1964, the French were
officially advocating the creation of the CRU. Although based essentially on the published ideas of
Dr. Edward Bernstein, the details of the proposal
were never explicitly spelled out publicly by the
French. Within the Group of Ten, the French delegation opted for an arrangement whereby the CRU would
have been linked directly with gold and distributed
to countries according to their gold holdings. The
new unit--not dollars--would then be transferred in
some constant proportion with gold in official international settlements of balance-of-payments deficits.

(The French suggested a ratio of nine parts gold to
one part CRU.) With the continued use of the dollar
as a reserve being a dead issue, U.S. deficits would
directly produce large gold losses and indirectly
instill discipline in the minds of U.S. policymakers. Equity and rationality would then be returned to the operation of the gold-exchange
standard.

Throughout 1963 and 1964, official French
thinking had been predicated on an acceptance of the
generally held proposition that the promised end of
the U.S. external deficit was imminent. This made
them amenable to the proposition that at some subsequent date the need would arise for an additional
source of international liquidity--one which would
bestow no special privileges or power on the United
States. Their preferred method of creating such
liquidity was a system designed to enhance gold and
emasculate the existing strength of the dollar. The
CRU was particularly well suited to this purpose.

By distributing the CRU's to countries solely
on the basis of existing gold stocks, the French
CRU proposal would have had the effect of increasing
the value of a country's gold stock and tying new
reserve assets to the volume of the world's monetary
gold. If enacted, the French CRU would have caused
a de facto increase in the price of the yellow metal.
This would have rewarded hoarders such as France and
penalized those countries with low gold ratios. The
reserve role of the dollar would be a dead issue,
and the United States would be subject to the same
balance-of-payments discipline as any other country.

THE ANTAGONISTS' POSITIONS REVERSED

One of the few touches of genuine irony and
humor which occurred during the international monetary reform exercise was the suddenness and totality
with which the two antagonists reversed positions in
1965. Divergent national interests in the United
States and France were explained to have inspired
diametrically opposed policies and objectives with
regard to the question of deliberate reserve creation. It is most ironical, therefore, that both
countries sharply reversed the course of their strategy with the peculiar and somewhat amusing result

that each country assumed the same general policy orientation discarded by the other. Indeed, each found it handy to use the other's now abandoned arguments in defending its new position.

After February, 1965, it was French policy to discount the wisdom of creating a CRU or any other new, international reserve asset. The United States, in July of that year, dropped its longstanding distaste for the concept of a new asset and replaced the French as its leading proponent. The net effect of this switch was a neat exchange of positions between France and the United States on the positive and negative poles of international monetary reform.

The French volte-face was decreed in an unexpected thunderbolt by President de Gaulle during his aforementioned February, 1965, press conference. In what must be ranked high on the list of the General's alltime surprises, he unequivocally called for a reversion to the nineteenth-century gold standard. France, he said, now felt that the international monetary system, as was the case before the great worldwide disasters, had to be established on an "unquestionably monetary basis which does not bear the mark of any individual country." He then explained how this could be done:

> Actually, it is difficult to envision in this regard any other criterion, any other standard than gold. Yes, gold, which does not change in nature, which can be made either into bars, ingots, or coins, which has no nationality, which is considered, in all places and at all times, the immutable and fiduciary value par excellence.[10]

The significance of de Gaulle's statement was to mark the formal politicalization of the international monetary reform talks. Into what previously had been an esoteric subject virtually ignored by all except government and academic economists, the substance of politics emerged from the shadows and periphery of the problem, settling firmly within its bloodstream. The monetary reform problem had been deemed too important and complex a thing to be left to economists by the highest political authority in at least one state. Involvement by other chief executives would follow. Once more, the General had

demonstrated his uncanny ability to see beyond the
horizon and instinctively spot exploitable situations before their true import had become apparent
to his counterparts elsewhere.

The political-economic motives behind de
Gaulle's pronouncement were a thinly disguised warn-
ing to the United States that it could no longer
take for granted Europe's continuing acceptance of
dollar liabilities. Neither could the United States
count on continued continental acquiescence in al-
lowing the United States to pursue foreign economic
and political policies without hindrance. Angered
by a monetary system which in his view had allowed
the United States to get away with financial murder,
the French President made it abundantly clear that
he wanted the United States to pursue policies within its own economic strength and that he felt the
sooner a European voice was able to speak up on
equal terms the better.

The exact timing of the General's initiative
can only be guessed at. It was traditionally
Gaullist to make decisions without consulting ministers, let alone the civil service staff. Furthermore, the General seldom felt the need for any
after-the-event accounting for his actions. The
best guess as to the French President's entrance is
that it was simply the climax of a long, behind-the-
scenes struggle for his favor by his unofficial
economic adviser, Jacques Rueff, and his Finance
Minister at that time, Giscard. Rueff's economic
philosophy was built on his genuine belief that a
U.S. balance-of-payments deficit and the dollar's
supremacy were undesirable but inevitable characteristics of the gold-exchange standard. As early as
1962, he made clear his beliefs that nothing short
of its systematic elimination and the reestablish-
ment of the discarded gold standard could eliminate
the unjustifiable and unfair benefits accruing to
this country. Rueff's distaste for this vehicle
of U.S. hegemony obviously was compatible with a
basic theme in de Gaulle's over-all foreign policy.

Throughout the first year of the monetary reform talks, however, the conduct of the French position had remained in the hands of the Finance Minister. Many of his differences with Rueff involved
only the question of degree. It will be remembered
that the former had introduced into the Group-of-Ten
studies the concept of a CRU which would be both

distributed and then used in strict accordance with
an unspecified ratio to gold. A country's gold holdings, not its dollar balances, would be its chief
means of balance-of-payments financing. Credit to
the United States would cease, and resulting gold
losses would at last enforce a discipline on the
United States similar to that always imposed on non-
reserve-currency countries. Nonetheless, the CRU
represented an attempt to introduce viable technical
changes within the monetary system's present structure. Giscard did not go as far as Rueff in wanting
to formally abolish the system in favor of an anach-
ronistic system abandoned after World War I and
somewhat incompatible with national commitments to
maximum domestic growth.

While the CRU was a viable economic device in
the minds of Bank of France and Finance Ministry
technicians, the Rueffian longing for a return to
the nineteenth-century gold standard where all payments deficits were settled in gold alone was shared
by the General as a useful diplomatic instrument.
Which of the two approaches was uppermost in official French policy depended mainly on the relative
influence of Rueff and Giscard. The General's
February, 1965, press conference indicated that the
former had finally won out.

The call for the return to the gold standard
was probably strategically timed to reinforce the
Bank of France's January, 1965, official announcement that it was immediately converting $150 million
into gold. The bank further announced that not only
would it continue the monthly conversions of $34
million (the price of thirty tons) initiated at the
end of 1963, but it would also begin converting automatically whatever new dollar balances accumulated
from France's continuing balance-of-payments surplus.
The result of this policy was the sale of $884 mil-
lion of gold by the United States to France in 1965.
This amount was more than twice the comparable figure
for 1964.

Bolstered by the leverage afforded by a persistent balance-of-payments surplus, President de Gaulle
was able to add a new dimension to his running quar-
rel with U.S. policies. The weakness of the dollar
and the vulnerability of the U.S. gold stock were
irresistible wedges with which to chip away at
the alleged excessive U.S. power and prestige. De
Gaulle's interest in the activities of the Group of

Ten was inevitable. Once he had asserted his unmis-
takable presence in the liquidity arena, French an-
tagonism toward the gold-exchange standard would
no longer be based on technical arguments. Neither
would French international monetary policy be characterized by moderation. A pronouncedly political
character and militant overtones were now the rule.

Michel Debre, who replaced Giscard as Finance
Minister in January, 1966, was particularly well
suited to carry forth the harsh Gaullist line. A
loyal Gaullist who was the first Prime Minister of
the Fifth Republic (1959-62), he had neither the
liberal suasion nor the economic background of his
predecessor. He was a lawyer by trade, and it was
widely reported that he had known very little about
the technical details of international monetary reform when he assumed the post of Finance Minister.

As voiced in public statements, the new French
policy was built on two arguments. First, the privileged position of the dollar had in fact terminated
the gold-exchange standard as such. Secondly, the
only permanent and rational monetary system would be
one based entirely on gold.

Debre provided a succinct summary of this dual
French argument in a speech delivered in Montreal in
January, 1967. He stated that the international
monetary system was "no longer a system based on the
gold-exchange standard; in fact, it is an international currency system based on reserve currencies
and more especially on one reserve currency, the
dollar, which represents the greatest economic force
in the world." He went on to say that a national
currency could be an adequate and impartial international reserve currency only if

> . . . the monetary authority re-
> sponsible for this currency were
> to sacrifice its own interests,
> when necessary, to the interests
> of the international community,
> considering its monetary policy
> in terms of international economic
> equilibrium rather than of its own
> requirements. But this is some-
> thing one cannot ask of any other
> country; there is no country that
> can easily, comfortably, and last-
> ingly subordinate the management of

its currency to the interests of
international equilibrium.[11]

After he had ruled out the dollar or any other
national currency what then could be used in making
international-payments settlements? Debre's answer
was gold. Upon reverting to a system based on gold,
Debre declared that at the same time it would be
necessary to settle all of the debts outstanding
from previous years (i.e., United States and United
Kingdom short-term liabilities to foreigners) and
also to provide for modern forms of credit among
nations. In a nutshell, the ideal international
monetary system for France was one in which official
exchange reserves essentially would be composed of
gold and where the financing by the central banking
authorities in deficit countries would be carried
out, apart from the use of credit facilities, by
movements of gold: "This is what one calls the gold-
standard system." The French position was fixated
with the notion that only gold was independent of
national powers, its issue being determined neither
by the balance-of-payments deficits nor the wishes
of any one nation.

In an interview in January, 1967, Debre explained
exactly under what circumstances France could go
along with the creation of a new form of monetary reserves. The first two preconditions which had to be
met were a disappearance of the deficits of the
reserve-currency countries and a collective determination that an international liquidity shortage
existed. This was a position fully consistent with
France's EEC partners.

But a third condition was added: New reserve
instruments could logically be created only if there
existed no "other means available to add to international monetary liquidities or to prevent the contraction thereof." What could be wrong in asking
that "a study of the advantages and disadvantages of
all solutions, without any taboos or exclusions, pre-
cede the adoption of any one of them?" The trust of
the French policy was thus directed to breaking the
"conspiracy of silence" which had prevented what they
felt to be an adequate discussion of the role and
price of gold in the international monetary system.

Debre never recommended an increase in the price
of gold except by implication. He always stopped

short of directly advocating such a move: "On this
question the position of the French authorities is
not a dogmatic but a pragmatic one. I have no a priori position as to the level at which the price of
gold should be fixed." He said he thought it necessary to analyze the facts and then draw conclusions
from the evidence that emerged.[12]

The French preoccupation with gold and their
repetitious attempts to force the rest of the Group
of Ten and the IMF, against their wills, to consider changing the role and price of gold as a means
of "reforming" the gold-exchange standard, produced
a state of near-total isolation of the French in
the monetary reform talks. Undismayed, France continued to adhere to a two-tier gold offensive
throughout 1965 and 1966. On the theoretical level,
its policy in the liquidity talks was to continue
opting for the elimination of the reserve-currency
role of the dollar--first by means of a CRU, secondly, by means of a reversion to the gold standard.
On the operational level, the Bank of France continued to convert dollars into gold. This was the
ultimate protest against both the power and privileges of the United States. The French, as well as
their EEC partners, recognized the fact that balance-
of-payments surpluses are politically valuable in
addition to being economically desirable: They tend
to shift power from the United States to the reserve
hoarders. But only France was prepared to engage in
brinksmanship and actually drain large amounts of
U.S. gold on a persistent basis. Whatever interest
earnings that country might have lost by holding
gold in lieu of interest-bearing dollar assets can
be reconciled as an expense of increasing French
power and influence relative to the United States.

That the U.S. Government did not take the
General's initiative lightly was confirmed in part
by a second February news conference. This time it
was President Lyndon B. Johnson's turn. Following
the General's gold initiative by a matter of just a
few days, the President hastily made public the soon-
to-be imposed set of measures designed to once and
for all restore equilibrium in the U.S.-payments
deficit. The new program, which was primarily aimed
at halting capital outflows, included provisions for
renewal and widening of the Interest Equalization
Tax, a voluntary program of restraint on direct foreign investments by U.S. corporations, and voluntary
guidelines on new overseas loans by U.S. banks.

For the next few months, U.S. policy was characterized by the attempts of the newly appointed
U.S. Treasury Secretary, Henry H. Fowler, and his
Under Secretary for Monetary Affairs, Frederick L.
Deming, to adjust to their jobs and by the efforts
of the entire government and business community to
digest the newly adopted sets of guidelines. A virtual moratorium now developed on U.S. initiatives in
the international monetary reform talks. The U.S.
delegation treaded water while strenuously resisting
French efforts to sink the dollar.

The shift in U.S. policy on monetary reform
was as abrupt and sudden as was the French. After
but three and one-half months in office, Secretary
Fowler reconsidered and then abandoned without warn-
ing the previously unwavering U.S. position that
an expansion of existing credit facilities was all
that the international monetary system needed. In
what otherwise would have been an obscure address
to the Virginia Bar Association, on July 11, 1965,
Fowler set out in search of a better world economy
and a new reserve asset.

He told his audience that, as authorized by
President Johnson, the United States now stood prepared to attend and participate in a multilateral
conference that would consider what steps could
jointly be taken to secure substantial improvements
in international monetary arrangements. Although
the Secretary indicated that his government was en-
gaged in an "intensive internal preparation" for
the meetings and negotiations which would follow,
he said the United States was "not wedded" to any
specific procedure or timetable. The absence of
an official reform plan was, no doubt, an outgrowth
of the fact that there had been only a very few days
between Fowler's personal decision that the United
States would take a positive stance on reform and
its public enunciation in his Hot Springs speech.

In the interim, he had little more than to obtain President Johnson's approval and have his staff
immediately prepare the text of the speech which
"fell like a bombshell" among domestic and foreign
finance officials alike. There were no advance
consultations with other members of the Group of
Ten or with the IMF. Neither in fact was there any
formal advance notice to other Executive Department

officials or even to Congress. One official explained that there had been an uncertainty in the
upper echelons of the Treasury Department as to
exactly when or in what form the Secretary's initiative would emerge from an interagency discussion.
Accordingly, advance consultations--even within the
U.S. Government--were virtually nonexistent. The
Secretary had made his decision and acted without
delay to pursue international monetary reform.

The reasons behind the 180-degree shift in
U.S. policy, by and large Fowler's personal decision, were fivefold. In his public pronouncement
of this change, Fowler referred to the "happy con-
currence of three crucial facts" which made the
time appropriate to act on reforming the monetary
system. The first of these reasons was a sharp improvement in the U.S. balance of payments and expectations that the two new programs of capital
restraint would serve to perpetuate this trend. In
February, 1965, the aforementioned wide-ranging
balance-of-payments program had been introduced.
Reflecting its effects, the U.S. balance of payments
which had suffered a deficit (measured on the liquidity basis) of $800 million in the first quarter of
1965 moved into a surplus position in the second
quarter. This was the first quarterly surplus since
1961, and there was much confidence that at last the
deficit was going to be ended. Some real apprehen-
sion about the consequences on future increments to
international liquidity of such a development then
began to develop within the government. Simultaneously, confidence in an improved U.S. bargaining
position blossomed.

A second factor was the completion of the technical phase of study. With the submission of the
Ossola report, the international monetary reform
exercise was at a major turning point. Now that
the major technical study phase was over, the Group
of Ten could either drop the whole project altogether or move into a more formal planning phase.
It was therefore an ideal time for a major initiative. The fact that the tone of the report indicated
that the consensus preferred a supplement to gold
and the reserve currencies rather than a substitute
for reserve currencies must have been especially
heartening and encouraging to the U.S. Government.

A third factor which Fowler cited was the
growing public (and official) opinion in the United
States that a new reserve asset was needed. The
widespread national support which greeted Fowler's
sudden switch suggests not only the validity of
this last assumption but also the power of public
and Congressional opinion. By mid-1965, a nearly
unanimous consensus which pervaded academia and the
executive and legislative branches of the U.S. Government held that nothing short of a new reserve
asset could adequately serve future liquidity needs.

Encouraged by Secretary Fowler's change in
policy, the Congressional Joint Economic Committee
published "Guidelines for Improving the International
Monetary System," in September, 1965. The report
stated that "the need for action is pressing. . . .
Increases in Fund quotas cannot, in themselves,
fully meet the needs of the future." The first of
twelve guidelines concluded that world-liquidity
needs could not adequately be met by existing sources
of reserves or even by the addition of new reserve
currencies. "New ways of creating international reserves must be sought." This was not a new position
for the Joint Economic Committee; as early as 1962,
it was urging the United States to take the leadership in establishing a mechanism which could regularly add to international reserves.

The President's Council of Economic Advisers
(CEA) had also taken a liberal position in contra-
distinction to Roosa's conservative, go-slow approach
to monetary reform. In the early 1960's, there was
considerable concern that the U.S. economy was operating well below its capacity, and emphasis was
placed on economic growth and reduced unemployment.
There was thus strong feeling within the CEA at this
time against having to impose deflationary restraints,
the traditional remedy for a persistent balance-of-
payments deficit. A liberal injection of liquidity
into the international monetary system was seen as a
logical way to circumvent the need to sacrifice domestic priorities for the sake of external-payments
equilibrium. In addition, the international special-
ist within the three-man council in the early Kennedy
years was James Tobin. A colleague of Robert Triffin's at Yale, Tobin was considered to be a general
adherent of Triffin's internationalist approach.

Even Roosa, whose international monetary ideas
had held sway with President Kennedy, had changed

his views by mid-1965, and his proposal for a fund
unit account, a reform plan not substantially different from Bernstein's CRU proposal, was published
in the fall.[13]

A fourth factor was one of timing: The IMF's
annual meeting was approaching. There was little time
to lose if there were to be the initial consultations,
called for in the Secretary's speech, in advance of
that meeting.

A fifth and critical factor was Fowler's revised
assessment of U.S. national interests and priorities
in mid-1965. After studying the international monetary situation closely, his conclusion was that the
real menace to the dollar was the increasing strain
on the entire monetary system which would result
from continued but hostile dependence on the U.S.-
payments deficit as the prime source of additional
liquidity. Expansion of traditional credit facilities was not enough, and the greatest danger of all
was in standing still instead of doing something.

In view of the U.S. commitment to international
monetary stability, and with the troublesome and persistent deficit apparently under control, the Treasury Department decided U.S. interests would best be
served by developing a new reserve unit as a supplement to the dollar. Such a unit would foster a
multilateral sharing of monetary responsibility while
simultaneously preventing otherwise fatal defects in
the gold-exchange system from getting out of hand.
In other words, the second basic cornerstone of U.S.
international monetary policy (the first being adequate liquidity for maximum economic growth) would
not now be jeopardized in any consideration of deliberate-reserve creation. In light of the Ossola
report, which found the French alone in supporting a
gold-linked CRU as the exclusive means of settlement
among central banks, the U.S. Treasury Department
believed that no "fundamental confrontation" with
the dollar's reserve role was likely in any international monetary reform negotiations. Support outside of France for an asset which might be designed
to overwhelm and supplant outstanding dollar balances
was discounted. The academic phase had adequately
shown a Group-of-Ten consensus favoring a substitute
for future increases in gold- and foreign-exchange
holdings, and not a substitute for existing dollar
holdings.

The United States, under Secretary Fowler's leadership, now devoted itself to achieving international agreement on a new asset which would supplement (not challenge) its $30 billion in outstanding dollar liabilities to foreigners and which would have no direct link to gold. Having "bitten the bullet," Fowler personally assumed much of the burden of stirring the Europeans into a similar state of concern and desire for positive action. At the end of August, the Secretary left Washington, D.C., for a two-week trip to Europe for conferences to sound out the thinking of his counterparts in France, Italy, Germany, Sweden, Belgium, the Netherlands, and the United Kingdom, in that order. He would return encouraged that the continental countries were prepared to further consider the subject of international monetary reform and confident that a U.S. initiative in this area could succeed.

The United States now felt a first class reserve asset was necessary to prevent the world from moving into an increasing web of restrictions and to establish the clear mechanism for adding to world reserves which would be necessary to prevent disruptive currency speculation. The United States would later argue that, in order to accomplish these objectives, the new asset would have to be "unconditional, nonrepayable, convertible into vehicle currencies, transferable, and separate from other IMF assets." The United States wanted the kind of asset which central banks would count in their reserves.

INTERNATIONAL LIQUIDITY POLICIES IN THE OTHER GROUP-OF-TEN COUNTRIES

Since U.S. and French interests would be the most affected by any reform of the monetary system, it is understandable that theirs were the most pronounced and diametrically opposed policies in the liquidity talks. Within the central portion of the monetary spectrum of thought rested the other eight in the Group of Ten. But of these eight, only Germany played a role of importance equivalent to France or the United States. With the exception of Italy, the remaining countries lacked either the power or the inclination to be major craftsmen in the creation of the new international reserve asset. Theirs was in general a supporting participation.

Germany was the final member of the triumverate which made the decisions in the reform talks. The Bonn Government does not fear or dislike U.S. political, military, or economic strength with anything approaching the intensity of its French neighbors. Indeed, the security of that country rests in no small degree on this power. Instead of Gaullist self-assertiveness, German foreign policy is characterized by a continued recognition of a need for allies. A feeling of solidarity and interdependence rather than a bent for independence and a whittling away of U.S. power is evident in this prosperous but troubled country. West German attitudes are inevitably affected by the deep insecurity of a country whose borders and former capital city are in limbo, and whose national identity still has not fully recovered from the Nazi experience and the ordeal of military defeat.

War guilt, the partition of the country in two sectors, and the absence of a charismatic leader like de Gaulle inevitably make German policy toward the United States different from that of the French. Rather than independence, the Germans, heretofore at least, have wanted to achieve only respectability and full equality with the middle powers of the Atlantic Alliance. Additionally, the country's situation and past make it perfectly willing to subsume its sovereignty in such multilateral organizations as the Common Market and the now defunct multilateral-fleet concept. The Germans profess neither de Gaulle's great power ambitions nor his rejection of great sacrificies of sovereignty.

German appreciation for U.S. power by no means implies that it unequivocally accepted either the U.S. balance-of-payments deficit or the nearly autonomous ability of this country to determine the volume of international liquidity. Both of these factors conflict with the values of German economic orthodoxy. It shares France's insistence that the U.S. deficit end, but not--at least in public-- France's basic criticism that the United States derives intolerable power and prestige by virtue of the dollar's role as a reserve currency.

German criticism of the dollar drain appropriately tends to be couched in purely technical terms. It is not illogical that a country whose economy at one point was all but destroyed by inflation should

focus its wrath on the alleged inflationary consequences of the U.S. balance-of-payments deficit. According to Karl Blessing, President of the Deutsche
Bundesbank (the German Central Bank), not even the
most ingeniously conceived international monetary
system can function satisfactorily without monetary
discipline. He told an IMF audience that under a
fixed exchange rate system, even countries with sound
monetary policies are forced to import inflation when
other countries don't maintain sufficient monetary
discipline. "Even a perfect machinery for financing
balance-of-payments deficits cannot replace domestic
adjustments. In financing deficits we should in the
future pay more attention to price stability than to
expansion and growth."14

The basic attitude of the Germans toward the
liquidity question remained constant throughout the
duration of the monetary reform talks. In determining the adequacy or shortage of liquidity, they felt
it necessary to take a macro or global view. As one
German official expressed it, what is important is
the worldwide need, not the needs of any one country
or any single group of countries (the latter probably
being the less-developed countries).

An excellent summary for this German view is
found in Blessing's address before the IMF's 1965
annual meeting. He claimed that if all leading countries would strive for balance-of-payments equilibrium, the need for reserves would be small. Temporary
deficits are almost inevitable, but could be financed
from owned reserves or from conditional reserves such
as those provided by the fund or other credit institutions. He stated: "I cannot help thinking that
too perfect a machinery for financing balance-of-
payments deficits weakens monetary discipline and
contributes to creeping inflation." His EEC colleagues could heartily subscribe to this basic argument. Germany saw no urgent need for additional
liquidity, especially since IMF quotas were being
increased considerably. The fact that some deficit
countries might be short of reserves could not itself justify a global increase of liquidity. He
further noted: "We cannot bring the tide to a higher
level because a few ships have run aground. To do
that would mean inflation pure and simple. Such
grounded ships must be refloated by making them
lighter." He also admonished against creating money
artificially to assist the developing countries.15

It has been a repeated German assertion that the disappearance of the U.S.-payments deficit would not lead to an immediate liquidity shortage. Nevertheless, that country since 1963 had been openly supporting the negotiation of a contingency plan for the introduction of a new international reserve asset. In the fall of 1965, Blessing noted that since no one could predict with certainty whether newly mined gold or Soviet gold sales would cover the world's liquidity needs in the future, Germany was prepared for further discussions in the Group of Ten in order to develop "in the foreseeable future suitable procedures and appropriate machinery to be used in case liquidity should really prove insufficient." The Germans, however, would consider it a mistake to create liquidity in anticipation of a need, since this would produce a "constant temptation to apply less monetary discipline."

Germany thus incorporated portions of both the French and U.S. positions. They foresaw no immediate liquidity shortage even after the end of the U.S. balance-of-payments deficit. Still, they felt that technical explorations of acceptable solutions were immediately necessary in view of the "considerable divergences of opinion" which existed between the leading Atlantic countries on the question of monetary reform.

The Germans, from the beginning of the reform talks, found that their own interests overlapped those of both France and the United States. In view of their close and valued relationship with both, it was obvious that Germany was not going to throw the full weight of her influence against either of her fellow members of the Atlantic triumverate. Nor did she need to. The German position genuinely contained roots from both her allies' positions. Germany shared the French distaste for the excesses of the gold-exchange standard. She believed the top international financial priority was a prompt and permanent restoration of equilibrium in the U.S. balance of payments. The Germans felt that a shortage of international liquidity was out of the question until well after that deficit had ended, and also that a clear distinction had to be made between agreement on--and activation of--a standby reform plan.

But at the same time, the Germans wanted to follow through with contingency planning. Acknowledging

the long process of reaching agreement on a new reserve asset and obtaining formal ratification, Dr.
Otmar Emminger, a member of the Bundesbank's Direc-
torate, said he considered it necessary to negotiate
well in advance of the "new situation" which was
being planned for. "No one can say in advance whether, within the several years which such planning
would presumably require, the said contingency might
not in fact appear." The Germans, unlike the French,
wished to build on the gold-exchange standard, not
dismantle it. They wanted to control the international role of the dollar, not destroy it.

     In late 1966, the over-all tone of German criti-
cism of the monetary system continued to be moderate.
The German outlook remained heavily influenced by
the need to work closely with the United States in
easing the foreign exchange costs to the United
States of its military presence in Western Europe.
In addition to continuing its policy of "offsetting"
direct expenditures, the German Central Bank in
April, 1967, officially notified the Federal Reserve
Board that it was prepared to continue indefinitely
its already existing albeit informal policy of not
using the dollars generated from its chronic balance-
of-payments surplus to purchase U.S. gold.

     German differences with the French were not only
procedural. They were also substantive. Blessing
noted that the Bundesbank fully agreed with the French
that "ways and means must be found to put an end" to
the creeping international inflation fueled by the
deficits of the reserve-currency countries and that
"creation of fresh international liquidity must be
linked with strict, multilaterally controlled rules."
But agreement with the French went no further. Their
ends might have been the same, but their means dif-
fered. "The German Federal Bank's standpoint differs
from the French not in the goal, but in the method.
In the German view the gold-exchange standard could
be improved and tightened so that it forms an efficient international monetary system."[16] Whereas
France had no use for reserve currencies, Germany
preferred retaining one or more "live" reserve currencies, provided that they were kept in sufficiently
short supply.

     It was Germany's over-all position that the
defects of the gold-exchange standard were not in
the system itself but in its application. True,

there had been excessive creation of dollar reserves, but no merit was seen in a return to the old gold standard which Germany felt logically had to entail an increase in the price of gold. Emminger said in January, 1967, that he was "terrified" when thinking about the inflationary effects of a doubling in the price of gold. Earlier, Blessing denied that such a "once-and-for-all" price increase would permanently solve the problem of international liquidity. Once the increase in liquidity had been absorbed, the problem would arise again after a certain lapse of time.

The essence of the German policy toward deliberate-reserve creation was support for a reserve unit to be designed and utilized under a relatively stringent set of controls. This would prevent its being abused by irresponsible deficit countries. Blessing's 1966 address to the fund's annual meeting emphasized two key points: "first, the interest of all countries in a smooth functioning of the international monetary system, and, secondly the responsibility of a limited group of major countries who in practice would have to provide a substantial portion of the financial backing for any new reserve assets." He also added that in planning such reserve assets, care should be taken that they "do not dislodge the dollar from its present position." Shortly before the fund meeting, Blessing had advised that if new reserve units were in fact created, they should be linked as closely as possible to gold, or at least carry a gold-value guarantee. He felt it would be desirable for the units to be transferable from one central bank to another only if accompanied by a certain proportion of gold.

The monetary reform policies of Italy, the Netherlands, and Belgium-Luxembourg were all but completely synonymous with the German position. Throughout the 1964-67 period, none of these countries felt there was any question of an existence of insufficient reserves or a threat of a worldwide deflation. They all felt that there were more important international monetary priorities than new reserve creation, which was viewed as only a long-range issue. The liquidity policies of these countries nevertheless accepted the need for contingency planning in advance of the problem, but on the absolute understanding that activation of any agreed-upon reform would be possible only in the event of a U.S.

balance-of-payments equilibrium and a general, worldwide scarcity of liquidity. Finally, all recognized
the "special responsibilities" of the major countries
in the preparation of a plan and in the process of
decision for its activation. The EEC countries were
simply unwilling to accept a process of decisionmaking which could ever systematically overrule them.

Throughout the postwar period, Italy did not
place a great deal of emphasis on external matters.
Preoccupied with over-all political instability and
economic growth, particularly in its underdeveloped
southern half, Italy did not have the aggressive
foreign policies of either France or Germany. The
country was, however, endowed with two extremely
competent economic technicians, Treasury Minister
Emilio Colombo and Guido Carli, one of the most respected central bank governors in the Atlantic community. Consequently, Italy pursued a monetary
reform policy based essentially on pragmatism and
strategic flexibility. At the heart of its policy
was the simple desire to see the Group of Ten reach
agreement on an effective standby reform plan. The
Italians were usually quick to offer suggestions and
compromises.

Although they dismissed the idea of any immediate need to supplement existing forms of liquidity,
the Italians did not wish to see any contraction in
the existing level of international liquidity, an act
resulting from an increase in the propensity of central banks to hold gold relative to reserve currencies, and/or the movements of foreign-exchange
reserves from low-gold-ratio to high-gold-ratio countries. To discourage further conversion of dollars
into gold (which would cause a net decline in U.S.
reserves and therefore in worldwide liquidity), the
Italians advocated a policy of "harmonization" of
reserve holdings. This approach suggested that high-
gold-ratio countries would settle deficits mainly in
gold and accumulate surpluses mainly in other reserve
assets, while low-gold-ratio countries would do the
opposite. In this way, total national reserves would
be brought, progressively and by stages, toward a
permanent average-gold to reserve-currency ratio
which would be established for those countries participating in the harmonization arrangement. Even
with the support of the Germans, however, the harmonization idea never gained enthusiastic acceptance (the
U.S. delegation, for example, argued the conceptual

impossibility of having this country, which could
not count dollars as reserves, hold reserve currencies in any large proportion to gold).

The Italians agreed with the principle that
deliberate-reserve creation should meet the needs
of the whole world, but, like the Germans, stressed
the need to have it accepted that the major industrial countries have "special responsibilities not only
in drawing up a contingency plan for reserve creation
but also in the decision regarding its activation."
Again echoing the Germans, Treasury Minister Colombo
told the 1966 IMF meeting that no scheme, decided
upon in advance of actual needs, should be activated
before the external deficits of the reserve-currency
countries were eliminated. Italian officials were
always quick to emphasize their nonrigidity on
strictly technical issues, which they rated secondary in importance. After all, they would say, the
fundamental issues involved in the process of reserve
creation "are essentially of a political nature."

Marius Holtrop of the Netherlands Central Bank
told the IMF's 1966 annual meeting that the monetary
reform talks should proceed "because the contingency
it would take care of is a potential threat that
should be removed." The Netherlands was "ready to
cooperate fully in the continuing studies aiming
toward the preparation of a contingency plan for the
possible creation of additional reserves as and when
needed."

But, like his German colleague, he felt that
a clear distinction had to be made between a contingency plan and the actual creation of additional
reserves, and that "an effective and equitable procedure for the taking of decisions on actual creation
should be established." Such a procedure would take
into account the general interest of all countries
as well as special interests and responsibilities
of a limited group of countries. Holtrop also added
that "deliberate creation of monetary reserves should
not have the purpose of bringing about a permanent
transfer of real resources from one group of countries
to another."

The Dutch representative said that he shared
the British preference "for a unit type of asset
over a drawing right type." In order to assure the
proper use of such units to preserve the functioning

of the adjustment process and to strengthen balance-
of-payments discipline, the Netherlands felt that
"the possible reform of the monetary system should
also contribute to enhancing the disciplinary function of gold." Dutch officials felt that this could
be achieved by providing for a transfer ratio linking
the use (but not the initial distribution) of a new
reserve unit to gold.

The Belgian delegate asserted to the IMF that
his country was still convinced of the usefulness
of technical discussions. Such studies "will be
of great importance for the political authorities
when, at a time and on conditions that cannot be
foreseen at the moment, they have to make decisions
in this field." At the 1965 IMF meeting, the Belgian
delegate suggested that liberalization of the IMF
could provide the basis of international liquidity
expansion: "If the gold tranche and the supergold
tranche could be given the legal status they deserve
and be therefore (a) an unconditional reserve and
(b) a real asset freely transferable to any other
member of the fund, they could be considered as good
as gold and incorporated in central bank reserves."
(Automatic accessibility to the gold tranche remained
a Belgian project throughout the negotiations.)

Throughout the reform talks, the strength of
the United Kingdom continued to be sapped by persistent balance-of-payments deficits and speculation
against the pound sterling. The country remained
heavily dependent on multilateral credit operations
to prevent a full-scale financial crisis. Hence,
British efforts to work for a liberal reform plan
were compromised by their precarious economic position. But what the British lacked in strength they
made up in positivism. Chancellor of the Exchequer
Reginald Maudling in 1962 had broken the ice of
official silence on the need to consider reforming
the international monetary system. One year later,
he attacked the apathy with which his initiative
was greeted; a thorough evaluation of the system
was "a matter of urgency," he said. Calling for
a pace which would produce "definite practical decisions" within a year, Maudling cautioned that results
were more important than methods. "It is important
to ensure that we do not spend so long looking for
the ideal solution that we fail to make progress on
improvements that can be made in the meantime," he
stated.

The British never publicly pushed for any specific reform plan; their efforts were on behalf of
liquidity creation in general. Almost anything to
bolster the beleaguered pound sterling and assist
in balance-of-payments financing would have been
welcomed with open arms. The United Kingdom was
"ready to consider with an open mind" all proposals.
The major prerequisite, stated the then Chancellor
of the Exchequer James Callaghan, was agreement itself. There would be no advantage to the world
should each country in the Group of Ten hold fast
to their own particular reform preferences "if the
result should be that we were not ready to meet the
need deliberately to create more reserves as that
need arises."

Throughout the final months of negotiations in
1967, the British role in the reform talks became
notably restrained as preparations were then beginning in earnest for the second British application
for membership in the Common Market. This was also
the period of an attempt by the EEC to adopt a
unified-consensus position, one quite distinct from
the liberal Anglo-Saxon position on monetary reform.
As The Economist caustically suggested, it would
have been less than tactful for the British to pour
"too much cold water on the budding flower of a
joint community position."17 At the climatic Group-
of-Ten ministerial meeting in July, 1967, chaired
by Callaghan, some of the delegates were reportedly
"fascinated" by the silence of the chairman and
the British delegation during the debate between
the United States and the six. The Financial Times
mused that it appeared as if instructions had "gone
out from a very high level to avoid at all costs
lining up with the Americans against the Common
Market."18

The liberal and positive attitudes of the two
Anglo-Saxon countries toward the concept of liquidity creation was fully shared by the other three
non-Common Market countries participating in the
Group of Ten--Canada, Japan, and Sweden. The substance and tone of the liquidity policies and
national interests of these five countries, devoid
of inflationary fears and gold-lined attempts to
harness the international political-economic power
of the United States were all noticeably different
from the conservative and negative views of the
EEC contingent in the Group of Ten. Rather than

reflecting the relatively negative preoccupation with
the U.S.-payments deficit and threats of inflation,
these attitudes were more concerned with the positive actions of making the system compatible with
economic growth. It is true, however, that none of
these countries were faced with the "burden" of prolonged dollar accumulations.

Both Japan and Canada are charter members of
what is termed the dollar bloc. Closely linked
with the economy of the United States and heavily
dependent on its capital market as a source of funds,
both countries continued to hold the bulk of the
foreign reserves in dollars throughout the 1960's.
Examples of their pressure on this country to restore payments equilibrium were virtually nonexistent. In fact, fear for their economic prosperity
inspired both to secure special exemptions from
official curbs on U.S.-capital outflows. Such a
concession would not have been forthcoming if either
Canada or Japan had adopted international financial
policies antagonistic to U.S. policies and objectives.

With specific regard to monetary reform, they,
like the Swedes, took for granted that the European
surpluses and propensity to buy U.S. gold with unwanted dollars had made necessary a new source of
international liquidity. In the words of the Japanese Finance Minister, Takeo Fukuda, adequate liquidity had to be provided to assure the future expansion
and prosperity of the world economy: "It would be
a matter of great regret if the absence of fundamental consensus about the future concerning international liquidity should lead various countries to
timid management of their economic policies, and
consequently to a contraction of the world economy."
The Japanese argued for the creation of new reserve
assets which would not be linked too closely with
gold.

The Nordic countries probably expressed the
least alarm over the impact and nature of the U.S.
deficit. Foreign trade accounts for as relatively
large a percentage of their gross national products
as it does in most EEC countries. But a lack of
the power-politics instinct has caused these countries to be totally apathetic with regard to the
need to accumulate gold or challenge the hegemonic
position afforded the United States by the gold-exchange standard. Consequently, they placed a great

deal of emphasis, as did the other non-EEC countries
in the Group of Ten on the positive aim of providing
adequate liquidity to assure continued expansion of
international trade.

During the IMF 1965 annual meeting, the Danish
Governor said that his part of the world was deeply
interested in the international monetary reform
talks, whose outcome he hoped would prevent either
a "general deflationary development or undesirable
disturbances created by speculative raids on important currencies." He opined that it would be
"most unfortunate if the influence of political considerations would lead to exaggeration of the difficulties" and prevent a satisfactory settlement. One
year earlier, at the 1964 meeting, the Norwegian
representative had argued that with a code of good
behavior on the part of the debtor countries well
established, there was an equally important need to
create a code of good creditor behavior. As a representative of a small country far more dependent
on foreign trade than most, he could not help but
wonder "why the Common Market countries that are so
afraid of importing inflation deem it necessary to
surround themselves with a trade wall of highly pro-
tective tariff barriers."

NOTES

1.   Charles O. Lerche and Abdul Said, Concepts
of International Politics (Englewood Cliffs, N.J.:
Prentice Hall, 1963), p. 7.

2.   Henry G. Aubrey, "The Political Economy
of International Monetary Reform," Social Research,
XXXIII (Summer, 1966), 240.

3.   Robert V. Roosa, Monetary Reform for the
World Economy (New York: Harper and Row, 1965),
pp. 25-26.

4.   Francis M. Bator, "International Liquidity: An Unofficial View of the United States Case,"
American Economic Association, Papers and Proceedings, LVIII (May, 1968), 620.

5.   "Remarks by the Honorable Henry H. Fowler, Secretary of the Treasury, before the Virginia State Bar Association, Hot Springs, Virginia, July 10, 1965," U.S. Treasury Department Press Release dated July 11, 1965, p. 6.

6.   Robert V. Roosa, The Dollar and World Liquidity (New York: Random House, 1967), p. 102.

7.   Ibid., p. 107.

8.   Ibid., pp. 6-7.

9.   Harold van B. Cleveland, The Atlantic Idea and Its European Rivals (New York: McGraw Hill, 1966), p. 84.

10.   "Excerpts from the Press Conference Held by General de Gaulle as President of the French Republic in Paris at the Elysée Palace on February 4, 1965," French Embasssy Press Release, February 5, 1965, p. 3.

11.   "Address delivered by Michel Debre, French Minister of the Economy and Finance before the French Chamber of Commerce of Montreal on January 13, 1967," Press Release of the French Embassy Press and Information Service, New York, pp. 1-2.

12.   "Interview: Michel Debre," The Banker, CXVII (February, 1967), 100.

13.   Roosa, Monetary Reform, op. cit.

14.   International Monetary Fund, "Summary Proceedings," Nineteenth Annual Meeting, 1964 (Washington, D.C.: The Fund, 1965), p. 53 (underscoring supplied).

15.   International Monetary Fund, "Summary Proceedings," Twentieth Annual Meeting, 1965 (Washington, D.C.: The Fund, 1966), p. 117.

16.   Bank for International Settlements, "Press Review," (Basle, Switzerland: March 10, 1965), p. 3.

17.   "Better than Nothing," The Economist, CCXXII (July 8, 1967), 138.

18.   Financial Times, July 18, 1967.

CHAPTER **4** THE MOVE
TOWARD CONSENSUS,
1966-67

In the eight months that followed the completion
of the deputies' report in July, 1966, the first
real movement toward consensus on international monetary reform imperceptibly began to materialize. It
was in this period that the critical process of political accommodation replaced the previously academic efforts to explore the various technical avenues
of approach.

THE POLITICAL DYNAMICS OF
NEGOTIATING MONETARY REFORM

The financial negotiators were not diplomats in
the classical sense. They were finance ministry and
central bank officials who were far less accustomed
than their foreign ministry colleagues to the machi-
nations of power politics. On the one hand, they
were all highly skilled members in the brotherhood
of a highly "scientific" discipline: international
finance. But on the other hand, they were also
politically responsive nationals of the United States,
France, Germany, Italy, Great Britain, Canada, Japan,
and the Benelux countries. Each of them possessed a
separate mix of values based on separate national
interests, and what they decided would directly affect the interests of their respective countries.

Although the concept of a sinisterly Machiavellian power struggle can be dismissed as an accurate
description of the monetary reform talks, several
very real political concepts--national interests,
sovereignty, power, strategy, and control--played a
central role. Between 1960 and 1965, a plethora of
private reform plans were advanced. Free from

concerns with negotiability and able to concentrate
on the economically ideal, many of these proposals
suggested revolutionary changes in the existing system. All were technically sound. But in disregard-
ing the politically feasible, these reform schemes
were visionary to the extent that they were devised
as optimum solutions to economic problems alone.
Econometric models depicting the technical excellence
of one plan over the other were not the basis of decisionmaking. Instead, decisions grew out of diplomatic bargaining which attempted to maximize national
value ends within a framework of compromise and
interdependence. Political acceptability, not economic logic, was the prime determinant of the direction taken by the financial diplomats.

That decisionmaking was a political process is
made clear in the succinct assertion by a key U.S.
participant that the liquidity talks could not properly be described as a panel of experts reaching
technical agreements, for there were "damn few technical questions." Substantive issues invariably had
to be formally approved at the cabinet level--or by
heads of state. One French official suggested during
the final stages of negotiation that only the wording
of the first page of the agreement was critical--that
was all the General would read. The making of an
international monetary consensus was not the stuff of
graduate school economics.

At the risk of oversimplification, the monetary
reform talks may be divided into two phases. The
first might be termed the academic-technical phase.
Lasting until mid-1965, this phase saw the deputies,
finance ministers, and central bank governors of
member countries in the Group of Ten, exploring a
vast, uncharted field of international economics.
There were few precedents and equally few absolutes
on which the deputies could base their study of the
need for and the means of deliberately creating a
new reserve asset. To begin with, no one was definitively prepared to say that he knew how much of
this new international reserve would be needed, when
it would be needed, or in what form it should be.

There were only nominal political overtones to
the initial phase. The deputies were not trying to
make conclusive recommendations. They were simply
trying to explore a virgin territory. Progress was
unexpectedly slow partly because of the newness of

the task of discussing international monetary reform
on an official, not academic, basis. A further
hindrance was the fact that of the participating
countries, only France had any preconceived policy
of how reform was actually to be brought about.
Furthermore, the United States was unenthused at best
about considering a major reform. As late as the
spring of 1965, a leadership vacuum at the Treasury
Department kept U.S. policy indifferent--even hos-
tile--to any material progress.

By the summer of 1965, the deputies had provided their ministers and governors with a wealth of
technical knowledge on deliberate-liquidity creation.
At the same time, however, the political will to reach
an agreement was all but nonexistent. President de
Gaulle in February had turned France in the direction of the nineteenth century with his call for a
return to the gold standard. A changing of the
guard had just been completed in the U.S. Treasury
Department. Neither Germany nor Italy had any strong
predispositions toward any single reform plan.

The very possibility at this point that further
liquidity planning would be shelved for lack of support was avoided only by the heroic efforts begun in
July by the new U.S. Secretary of the Treasury, Henry
H. Fowler. Suddenly and unexpectedly, the United
States reassessed its interests and became the ardent
supporter of not only a prompt agreement, but a far-
reaching and liberal one as well. With the introduction of U.S. initiative on behalf of a liberal
asset, the politicalization process begun the previous February by President de Gaulle's call for
the gold standard's return was formally underway.

The introduction of this second phase of the
talks was further marked in September, 1965, as ministers and governors of the Group of Ten once again
requested their deputies to explore what basis of
agreement could be reached on new arrangements for
the "future creation of reserve assets." The third
and most sophisticated technical paper was presented
to the ministers and governors in July, 1966. A
major plateau had been reached.

For almost three years, the delegates of ten
countries, prepared only by an earlier tradition of
close economic cooperation and consultation, had
studied and discussed the unique question of creating

monetary reserves with, in essence, nothing but
the stroke of a pen. There was really little left
to study at this point. The perimeters of action
were somewhat circumscribed. Only a political decision could determine if and how further efforts
would be made to reach an agreement. The far-reaching academicians' suggestions served to ignite a
public debate and construct a framework for official
thinking, but they attracted only limited sponsor-
ship in the councils of the Group of Ten, where the
premium was on preserving and serving national interests, not on economic excellence.

It seemed increasingly certain in mid-1966 that
the eventual outgrowth of the monetary reform deliberations would be some variation on the basic theme
of new reserve units. The successive settlement of
the large-issue areas in 1966 and 1967--the new
asset's link to gold, the width of membership in the
plan (Group of Ten versus universality), the role of
the IMF, and, finally, the rules of decisionmaking--
was the story of the successful evolution of the monetary talks. In some cases, one decision inevitably
led to another. For example, the July, 1966, agreement to assure the full participation of all IMF member countries in the reform plan all but eliminated
the possibility of any direct link between the new
asset and gold and entirely eliminated a two-pronged
U.S. plan to provide the Group of Ten with reserve
units and the entire fund membership with new, unconditional drawing rights in that organization. But
in most cases, agreements followed old-fashioned,
painstaking, political negotiation and compromise.

If our thesis is correct, i.e., that the monetary reform exercise was an aspect of Atlantic-
community politics and reflected a resurgent Western
Europe demanding a shift in the international monetary balance of power to its favor, then it must now
be demonstrated that traditional Atlantic political
patterns dictated the conduct and conclusion of the
monetary talks.

Because it was in no one's interests to simply
wait for the inevitable liquidity shortage without
having preplanned for the contingency, the talks did
in fact slowly move into the formal-negotiating stage.
It was here that France witnessed the final fade of
its dream to promote gold and demote the dollar. Its
proposal to create a CRU to act as the sole supplement

to the precious metal in international reserves
simply generated no support from any other quarters.
Neither did its later advocacy of a return to the
gold standard. Because the intents of the rest of
the Group of Ten were not nearly so blatantly political and invidious as were France's, they were
resolute in opposing the French preoccupation with
gold. As this opposition grew, France's reflex action was to increase its level of opposition to the
creation of any new reserve asset. Throughout the
academic phase, France and the United States had
been on opposite ends of the spectrum. This was
also the case in the political stage. But with the
compatibility of a new reserve asset with reserve
currencies seemingly assured, the two countries now
had reversed their positions on the poles of policy
toward international monetary reform.

Germany, Italy, and the Benelux countries were
carrying on no vendetta against the U.S. dollar.
But neither did they share the liberal, expansionist,
and internationalist views so prevalent in the
Anglo-Saxon countries. Economic growth and full employment were less important than was stability.
They agreed with the United States that a new form
of credit would eventually have to be introduced,
and they were determined to create a viable and efficient new reserve asset to supplement both gold and
reserve currencies, but only at the time that the
end of the U.S.-payments deficit produced a need for
an alternative source of monetary reserves. Germany,
Italy, and the Netherlands found the workings of the
gold-exchange system unacceptably biased in favor of
the United States. They did not wish to perpetuate
it, but, unlike the French, they had no desire to go
back and destroy all vestiges of the U.S. and
British "windfall." The view of the countries which
formed the international monetary balance of power
was masterfully summarized by Otmar Emminger as he
asserted that Germany would be satisfied to have U.S.
private and official dollar liabilities level off
and show no further major increases. "We do not
look so much to the past; we look to the future, and
what we want is that there not be any further lax
policies based on the gold-exchange standard. In
our view, the expansionary phase of the gold-exchange
standard is a chapter that we have concluded."1

Pursuit of value maximization in a milieu of
conflicting political and economic interests is the

stuff of politics. This pursuit was essentially
conducted by the three powers of the North Atlantic
area. Atlantic-community politics is recognizable
by Franco-American hostility, German-American cordiality, Franco-German unity, and the EEC's desire to
join hands in collectively asserting members' influence in Atlantic issues involving strategy and control.

Three interlocking sets of national interests
functioned in the international monetary reform
exercise. On the one side was the obdurate U.S.
insistence that a maximum reserve unit had to be
created in a minimum of time. Reflecting its status
as a debtor country with a deep commitment to rapid
worldwide economic growth and unfettered international
economic intercourse, the United States unflinchingly
sought a reform plan which could inject ample amounts
of a new form of liquidity free of any ties to gold,
compatible and not competitive with outstanding
dollar liabilities, and considered a full-scale,
unconditonally accepted means of settling balance-
of-payments deficits. With no slight resemblance
to the French CRU offensive begun three years earlier,
the United States had become the indefatigable and
insistent protagonist of the pressing need to reach
prompt agreement on a means of creating a new international reserve asset.

On the other side, directly challenging the
U.S. position, was the French monetary policy.
Reminiscent of the pre-July, 1965, U.S. policy
that argued consideration of a new asset was not
the proper avenue in which to channel efforts to
improve the international monetary system, the
French line trumpeted a return to the gold standard
and an eventual increase in the price of gold as the
most efficient course of action. Throughout 1966
and well into 1967, the French position centered
entirely around the precious yellow metal.

The total absence of support from any other member in the Group of Ten notwithstanding, the French
obstinately talked of the gold standard's glories,
while actively converting surplus dollars into gold.
Although France may have no leverage to change U.S.
policies on the control of nuclear weapons, its position through 1966 as a chronic balance-of-payments
surplus country gave it great leverage to influence
U.S. policies in the international financial field.
More than any other country, France invoked the

commitment of the U.S. Treasury Department to sell
gold at the fixed price of $35 an ounce to foreign
monetary authorities. Gradually converting into
gold previously accumulated dollar balances, and
after January, 1965, all new accumulations of dollars, the Banque de France by the end of 1966 retained only a nominal working balance of dollars
(about 10 percent of total reserves). Within these
two years, France's gold holdings increased by $1.5
billion.

The French, fearing the loss of some of this
leverage once a reform plan had been formulated,
were opposed even in principle to the continuance of
contingency planning. Unable to move any of their
Common Market partners to this position, but not
wanting to walk out on, or to bar the continuation
of, the reform talks, the French Finance Minister
insisted that his country could not fully participate
until the Group of Ten actively considered the
feasibility of using gold as the sole instrument of
international monetary transactions. The French
tactics were clearly designed to slow down the progress of the talks. Incessantly, they insisted that
a return to the gold standard, possibly coupled with
an increase in the price of gold, was a legitimate
means of improving the monetary system, and, as such,
had to be considered in as much detail as any alternative plan. The "conspiracy of silence" on the
central role and price of gold had to be broken.

The French never duplicated in the Group of Ten
their "empty-chair" tactic employed during their
1965 boycott of the EEC's institutions. But in limit-
ing their presence to an advocacy that the talks be
expanded to include consideration of the increase in
the gold price as a means of providing additional
liquidity, the French were temporarily nothing more
than de-facto participants.

By January, 1967, the isolated French position
was not only "untenable," it also had the effect of
antagonizing everyone else, including the other four
Common Market participants in the Group of Ten.
France's position had actually become counterproduc-
tive. Its gold blusterings had eventually served to
catalyze and enhance the support for progressing
with contingency planning by these four monetarily
conservative (by U.S. standards) countries.

The connecting link between U.S.-French polemics was the centralist policies pursued by the critical balancers of power in the international monetary
reform talks: the Germans, Italians, and Dutch. These
vital "swing" countries shared France's jaundiced
view of continued U.S. monetary hegemony, its lack
of boundless faith in paper currency, its insistence
that the U.S. balance-of-payments deficit had to
end, as well as its fear that an overabundance of
liquidity was in part responsible for exporting international inflation to the surplus countries. These
countries further shared France's insistence that the
power and influence of the surplus continental countries in international financial matters should be
commensurate with their economic strength. But theirs
was a rebuff to the dollar's omnipotence in the best
tradition of cordial alliance diplomacy.

France's Common Market partners had quickly
reached a nearly total convergence of views on the
basic issues of deliberate-reserve creation. They
all agreed that this problem was of a long-range
nature and that already existing, short-term credit
facilities and support arrangements were sufficient
to meet sudden tensions within the system. In addition to their unanimous preference for the limited
group approach, Rinaldo Ossola indicated they supported activation of a reform plan only in a situation of "a generalized scarcity of reserves" and
only after a better balance-of-payments equilibrium,
particularly by reserve-currency countries, had been
reached.

Standing strategically in between the extreme
French and U.S. positions, the other EEC countries
felt no strong commitment to either a quick breakthrough or a quick breakup of the talks. They shared
neither the French hostility against, nor the U.S.
preoccupation for, reaching agreement on a contingency
plan. They were swayed neither by the French desire
to return to the past, nor by the U.S. engrossment
with the future. Although they shared an unqualified
acceptance of the view that future reserve needs would
eventually dictate the need for deliberate creation
of a new asset, they were preoccupied, like the
French, with excessive U.S. deficits and privileges.
The deflationary dangers of a post-U.S. balance-of-
payments deficit period were regarded as distant.
The pressing priority was to halt their unwanted dollar accumulations. Such a development by itself would,

in the Europeans' thinking, constitute a reform of
the monetary system.

The balancers of international monetary power
formed concentric circles with the antagonistic
positions of France and the United States. Without
too great a shift in their policies, they could have
decisively tipped the delicate structure of the
negotiations in either direction. The immediacy of
Germany's, Italy's, and the Benelux countries'
association with France, together with the remote-
ness of a liquidity shortage, kept the prospect of
agreement on a reform plan in suspense until the
very last minute.

The most important country of the "swing" group
was West Germany. When it came to formally making
final decisions, the collective wills of the three
leading Atlantic powers--the United States, West
Germany, and France--predominated. The Germans were
strategically well-situated to mediate in the Franco-
American standoff. In the first place, they wanted
an agreement on an international monetary reform plan.
Secondly, the fact that Germany is economically the
most powerful country in the EEC gives it a political
voice which is respected by France and the United
States alike. Thirdly, Germany maintains extremely
close ties to both of these countries. European
geopolitical realities preserve the spirit of former
Chancellor Konrad Adenauer's emphasis on Franco-
German rapprochement, but national security considerations dictate a close and friendly alliance with the
United States.

The policymakers of the U.S. Government are
well aware of this country's "special relationship"
with Germany, and were not adverse to using it as a
means of minimizing de Gaulle's imprint and influence
on Western Europe. The liquidity talks were not unlike Atlantic military cooperation in this respect.
Beginning in the spring of 1967, the Treasury Department's leadership discovered the value of their close
allies and would indeed launch an all-out assault on
the German's innate Atlanticist orientation. Prolonged bilateral contacts would include not only
economic arguments but an expression at one point of
a U.S. fear that liquidity shortages resulting from
an inability to reach agreement on creating a new reserve asset could ultimately force countries to the
point of their having to cut back on outlays for

security. In other words, an "agonizing reappraisal"
loomed in the aftermath of any collapse of the liquidity talks.

A final but most critical dynamic of Atlantic-
community politics is the recurring attempt of the
six EEC countries to formulate a common policy vis-
à-vis the external world in international organizations. A sharing of basic economic and political
values has facilitated an unprecedented degree of integration and interpenetration in the European community. But this process has in turn spawned such
an extensive subculture of folklore, e.g., economic
spillover into politics.

Six countries founded the EEC, not out of aes-
thetics or disdain for self-determination, but as a
means of serving national interests. It was recognized, to a certain extent, that the traditional, independent, sovereign state could not keep up with the
demands of modern technology. But the fact is that
participation in that organization remains a means and
not an end in itself. Most of the initial euphoria
and optimism which greeted this new attempt at economic integration was wiped away by de Gaulle's cynical
attempts to use the EEC as a major vehicle for national enhancement. Structural policy differences still
threaten to splinter the fabric of the EEC, even after more than ten years of cooperation. This admit-
tedly oversimplified interpretation is probably far
more substantive than the popularly held notion of
six states operating on a new plateau of cooperation
and harmony while all the while peeling away layer
after layer of sovereign prerogative.

The Common Market assuredly has had many economic
successes. Adoption of both internal free trade and
a common external tariff have proceeded with unpredictable speed. All efforts at economic integration
notwithstanding, there is still no sign whatever,
wrote Raymond Aron, of an "irresistible or irrevers-
ible evolution from the Common Market to a European
unity comparable to a national unity."[2] In short,
no fatality of federalism yet exists. Six countries
are tending toward a commercial unity, not an economic
one, and still less to a political unity.

If it were indeed a resurgence of continental
political and economic strength which demanded a
voice equal to the United States in international

monetary decisionmaking denied by the machinery of
a dollar-dependent gold-exchange standard, then both
the strengths and weaknesses of the major platform
of that strength, the EEC, might be expected to be
visible during the monetary reform exercise. The U.S.
inability to overcome or sidestep unified EEC positions, once taken, exemplified the strengths. The
rancorous efforts to adopt these common positions
and the ability of France to portray the tail that
wagged the dog were examples of the weaknesses. Unable to simply send a single community negotiator,
as was done in the case of the Kennedy Round of tariff talks, to the Group of Ten, the EEC had to hold
a series of meetings where unity of international
monetary policy could only be achieved by bilateral
Franco-German accords. The latter were tangible
testament to France's ability to use the bugaboo of
EEC (or Franco-German) solidarity to advance and impose French objectives, shared by none of the other
member countries, which might have been totally dismissed if France had been participating in the Group
of Ten as a free agent.

The Treaty of Rome (which established the EEC)
contains no stipulation that the six should adhere
to a common policy on international monetary matters.
Despite this absence of a legal obstacle or the threat
of a French veto, there was no indication given that
Germany, Italy, or the Benelux countries were prepared to negotiate a contingency plan if the French
were either opposed to or absent from the continuing
talks. At the same time, France did not appear ready
or anxious to proceed unilaterally without its
partners.

It has been suggested by Stanley Hoffman of
Harvard that the Atlantic community is a true international community only in the loosest sense of the
term, and might more appropriately be referred to as
a "partial international system," with a true com-
munity--the EEC--developing within this system. According to this thesis, there are actually two major
layers, or strata, of relations operating within the
Atlantic area. The first is the classical interplay
of nation-state policies, in this case the predominance of one superpower over its weaker allies. The
second stratum represents those relations in which
some of the actors are not only states but also are
the members of a specialized in-group, the EEC.[3]

This concept was indeed elevated to the operational plane in the form of a series of meetings held by the finance ministers and central bank governors of the EEC. All paid special attention to formulating a common position for presentation to the Group of Ten. What in fact was happening in the fall of 1966 was the emergence of a subgroup within the Group of Ten. With the liquidity talks moving out of the academic, technical stage and into the political, decisionmaking phase, the six began taking steps to compromise their differences within a community body in order to insure that they spoke with a single point of view in the Group of Ten. It would be within the Common Market's finance ministers' meetings that some of the most critical decisions in the monetary reform exercise would be made.

AVENUES OF APPROACH IN EARLY 1966

In what was essentially a repetition of their studies held two years previously, the deputies once again, at their superiors' bidding, began a series of monthly meetings to consider further the question of how to reform the monetary system. The deputies resumed their meetings in November, 1965, under a new chairman, Otmar Emminger. He has been a member of the Board of Governors of the German Central Bank since 1953, and his main interests lie in the international sector. With two years of experience and two published reports on the subject as a background, the ten-country delegations plunged into relatively advanced discussions on international liquidity. It had been the hope of the optimists, such as Secretary Fowler, that a basic, meaningful agreement could be reached by the deputies sometime in the spring of 1966. But this would not be the case.

The first major development in the new round of talks came in January, when Chairman Emminger presented a plan designed to please both continental and United States demands. Quickly dubbed the "Emminger Compromise," the plan allegedly represented the views of Germany, Italy, the Netherlands, and Belgium. A cross between the more expansionary visions of the United States and the more conservative continental views, the plan had been worked out earlier in the Common Market's Monetary Committee.

The latter, like all of the principle Common Market
bodies, had been boycotted by France since June,
1965. Hence, France had neither approved nor rejected the proposal.

The Emminger Compromise received its first formal consideration at a deputies' meeting held in
Paris at the end of January. The first of the plan's
four main points was that the new reserve asset would
be created within a restricted group. Rather than
be distributed to all IMF members, the asset would
be restricted to the Group of Ten, or perhaps to all
those countries having strong, convertible, and usable
currencies. In addition, the Emminger Compromise
envisioned the new asset's being handled by the fund
in a separate account.

Thirdly, there was a compromise on voting procedures. Unanimity would be required for such "basic
issues" as the setting up of the mechanism of the new
asset, but year-to-year decisions could be decided
by a weighted majority. Finally, Emminger's plan
rejected the French proposal to link the distribution
of the new unit to existing gold holdings. Also
avoided was France's proposed ban on holdings of foreign exchange and the compulsory imposition of certain rations of gold and CRU's in reserve holdings.
The plan did suggest that there be a fifty-fifty link
between gold and the new reserve asset in the actual
financing of external-payments deficits. Unlike the
French proposal, this ratio would apply only to actual transfers and not to the distribution or holdings
of the new asset.

At this same January meeting of the deputies,
the Emminger Compromise was joined by the first formal exposition of a U.S. plan for international
monetary reform. Buried inconspicuously in the middle of the just-released Economic Report of the
President to the Congress, the plan involved a dual
approach. It reflected both the U.S. respect for
the continental demand for a limited-group approach
and its own desire to accommodate the interests of
the rest of the world. The U.S. plan paid deference
to both groups of countries by proposing two different reform techniques: a special drawing right
in the IMF and an entirely new international reserve
unit. In such a manner, it was suggested the "special needs and characteristics" of the industrial,

semi-industrial, and less-developed countries would
all be served.

The proposed new drawing rights would simply
expand automatic drawing rights in the fund. Because
they could be used merely on a declaration that a
country had a present need, these automatic but repayable drawing rights would become part of the reserves of all member countries.

The new international reserve unit, in contrast,
would be distributed only to a limited group of industrial countries. Backed by a guarantee against
depreciation in terms of gold, the unit in effect
would be a composite obligation of those countries
which had deposited balances of their national currencies in a common pool, held by a trustee, e.g.,
the IMF. Each participant would receive units as
part of its owned monetary reserves.

The initial public explanation of the new unit's
qualities showed that most basic things remained unchanged in the U.S. approach: Any new asset that
might be created should clearly be attractive enough
so that countries would want to hold it. "But it
must not be so attractive as to displace existing
forms of reserve holdings, for it would then fail in
its primary purpose of adding to over-all liquidity."[4]

Any rigid link between gold and the new asset was
"clearly undesirable." Such a link would provide incentives for all countries to increase the ratio of
gold to total reserves. "By thus affecting the
willingness of countries to hold existing reserve
currencies, it could lead to an undesirable shrinkage
in world liquidity." The Emminger idea of a link only
in the use of the asset was also dismissed because
any rigid link with gold "would tend to enhance the
importance of gold in the monetary system, and thereby assign a new reserve unit second-class citizen-
ship."[5] Several suggestions were included in the
President's report to provide assurances that the
new reserve unit, minus a gold link, would be readily
acceptable to participating countries.

The U.S. plan also suggested a targeted annual
growth of at least $2 billion in aggregate interna-
tional liquidity. Such a figure would maintain the
average annual increase in the fifteen year period

before 1965, a time when "there is little to suggest" that total liquidity increases had been excessive.

The French delegation maintained a nearly total
silence throughout the January deputies' meeting which
considered the Emminger Compromise and the U.S. plan.
Some interpreted this silence as a loss of interest
by de Gaulle in his gold-standard plea. This "cool-
ing off," together with France's growing isolation
in the liquidity talks, would, under this theory,
lead to a less intransigent and more compromising
French position.

But, once more, the ominous shadow of the General
would reenter the picture and dispel fond hopes for
a quick compromise settlement. A special French
interministerial strategy meeting to plot the French
position was held on February 25, 1965, in the Elysée
Palace. In "grunts and monosyllables," General de
Gaulle indicated that the analysis of the working of
the monetary system he had made at his famous press
conference of February 4, 1965, still expressed his
views on the subject.

De Gaulle's instructions to his financial people
were reported to have reiterated that gold was the
one and only valid foundation for the international
monetary system, and that since there was presently
no liquidity shortage, reform talks were completely
unnecessary and unjustified. That said, the French
delegation to the Group of Ten was to retain a modi-
cum of flexibility to the extent of simultaneously
denouncing the "inanity" of the liquidity proposals
which were being discussed, but still remaining within
the group and taking part in its meetings. French
tactics would be to stall for time while avoiding
either an agreement or a collapse of the talks.

In addition, President de Gaulle dismissed all
schemes for creating a new reserve asset. Thus was
buried the CRU. Once the official French plan advanced by ex-Finance Minister Giscard, the CRU became
a discarded and discredited French policy. Permeating
de Gaulle's statement was the notion that only an
increase in the price of gold would be a satisfactory
method of providing the additional liquidity which
might be needed at some future date.

During the meeting, one official had suggested that the French had more to lose than to gain in taking a completely negative stance on the need to increase liquidity. He went on to hint that the French might better support some liberalization of fund drawing practices rather than continue their refusal to acknowledge the need to plan for increased liquidity until well after the end of the balance-of-payments deficits of the reserve countries. He apparently hoped to soften de Gaulle's insistence that the monetary system should be based almost exclusively on gold. However, the plea for moderation was flatly rejected.

The French would henceforth cloak themselves in a hard, uncompromising Gaullist line of thinking--a politician's, not an economist's outlook on the international monetary system. As Finance Minister Debre said after the meeting, "the odds are that a council presided over by General de Gaulle will adopt General de Gaulle's ideas." And so it did.

At the second 1966 meeting of the deputies, the new French intransigence made itself felt. In a short statement, the French delegation repeated its country's view that the monetary system could be based only on gold. They added that an essential preliminary to any reform of the system, and in particular to any creation of new reserve units, was the restoration of equilibrium to the U.S. balance of payments. Each of the other principal delegations then nonchalantly went on to present technical notes on their earlier papers.

An open breach was averted at the meeting, and the French did not formally withdraw from the deputies' discussions. But, in effect, forward momentum had been halted, and the discussions were pushed back from consideration of what was negotiable to the earlier stage of debate on general principles and preliminary positions. The timetable for reform was clearly given a setback. Speculation quickly arose that whatever report emerged from the deputies would only be signed by nine countries.

Determined to push ahead despite the French obstinance, the deputies held another meeting in April, in Washington, D.C. Afterward, Deputy Chairman Otmar Emminger held a press conference. To seek ways and means of improving the international monetary system, said Emminger, is a long-run exercise.

It could be, over the long run, that an "insufficiency
of reserves will have disadvantageous effects and
will produce unsatisfactory national policies." The
urgency of finding the right kind of reserves for the
world, according to Emminger, was "to some extent a
function of the development of the U.S. balance of
payments." For as long as there were a sizable U.S.
disequilibrium, there would be enough reserves for
the rest of the world.

A major unresolved issue was the form the new
asset would take, the choice being between IMF drawing rights and a new reserve unit. Other unresolved
questions included the link between gold and the new
reserve unit as well as when and how to expand the
reform talks into a "wider body of discussion." Emminger confessed that he expected that "on some points
we won't get an entirely agreed report." Never men-
tioning France by name, he added that the deputies
would not get unanimity. They would simply inform
the ministers about majority views and minority reser-
vations. After that, "it reaches the stage of
political decisions."[6]

Should there in fact be "differences of opinion,
then they must finally be resolved on the political
levels, that is to say, by ministers and primarily by
the governments themselves, but the governments cannot really form themselves an opinion on any possible
disagreements without having a very good, well
reasoned report on where we agree, where there are
still disagreements, what are the reasons for the
disagreements, etc." It was this guide to official
thinking on monetary reform that would form the
basis of the deputies' report.

The deputies had started their second round of
meetings in an aura of optimism. Many had thought
it possible for them to reach agreement on recom-
mending a compromise plan by June, the due date of
their second report on the liquidity needs of the
monetary system. Long before their scheduled completion date, however, it was obvious that the schism
between France and the other nine participating countries would preclude any unanimous agreement on even
the most rudimentary technical aspects of monetary
reform. Indeed, France prevented unanimity on the
seemingly innocuous question of the need to consider
and construct a standby plan.

THE HAGUE CONFERENCE
OF THE GROUP OF TEN

The ministerial meeting of the Group of Ten
held in The Hague, July 25-26, 1966, was a major
turning point in the history of international monetary reform. It was this meeting which formally
opened the way for progression past the technical
study phase to one of full-scale negotiations. Furthermore, these negotiations would now be expanded
to allow participation beyond the Group of Ten to
include representatives of the more than ninety other
IMF members. Less than one year later, these "universal" negotiations would accomplish something that
three years of prior efforts could not: agreement in
principle on the draft outline of a contingency plan
for monetary reform.

The Hague meeting was characterized by the usual
conflict between French and U.S. polemics. The United
States again urged that standby machinery for deliberate-reserve creation be established as quickly as
possible. Treasury Secretary Fowler, from the start,
maintained his position that the Group-of-Ten talks
must be expanded immediately so that the ten would
not appear to be dictating the nature of monetary reform to the rest of the world. On the other hand,
French Finance Minister Debre's audience was visibly
irritated with his vehement renunciations of any need
for contingency planning.

The Italians, Germans, Dutch, and Belgians
pressed the U.S. delegation to agree on some formula
whereby control of the decisionmaking process in any
reform plan would be retained by a limited group of
strong-currency countries. To accomplish this objective, it was suggested that the facilities of the
General Arrangements to Borrow (GAB), over which the
Group of Ten has complete authority, be extended. The
United States argued that it would be politically
embarrassing to try to keep Group-of-Ten control over
decisions affecting the entire world's economic well
being. The United States refused to accept the European counter argument that the special position of
the strong-currency countries was already recognized
in the weighted voting procedures provided for by the
IMF Articles of Agreement.

What emerged from the disagreement was the vague
wording of the communiqué which said that in any
arrangement for a reform plan, the "requisite majorities and voting procedures" must give due recognition to "the particular responsibilities of a limited
group of major countries with a key vote in the functioning of the international monetary system and
which in fact must provide a substantial part of the
financial strength behind any new asset." One delegation, the French, was recorded as not being in
agreement with the views of the above section. Since
the communiqué also said that "there should be a
clear distinction between the establishment of any
contingency plan and the activation of that plan,"
France's abstention reflected its firm policy of formally disassociating itself from even the concept of
planning.

The communiqué issued after the ministerial
meeting again noted that the ministers and governors
"were in full agreement that there is at present no
general shortage of reserves." Once again there
followed the inevitable dictum that since neither
gold nor U.S.-payments deficits would supply sufficient sources of liquidity in the long run, "existing
types of reserves may have to be supplemented by the
deliberate creation of additional reserve assets."

The most important sections of the communiqué
dealt with provisions for non-ten countries. The
ministers agreed "that deliberately created reserve
assets, as and when needed, should be distributed to
all members of the fund on the basis of IMF quotas or
of similar objective criteria." Furthermore, in in-
structing their deputies to continue their studies on
the unresolved liquidity questions, they "thought it
appropriate to look now for a wider framework in which
to consider the questions that affect the world economy as a whole. With this in view, the ministers and
governors, after consulting with the managing director
of the fund, recommended a series of joint meetings
in which the deputies would take part together with
the executive directors of the fund."[7] The non-ten
fund members were finally given full access to the
reform talks.

Again, another report was called for; this one
was to be submitted by the deputies by the middle of

next year. "One delegation did not join in making
this aforementioned recommendation," the communiqué
advised.

The Europeans also reinforced their demand that
the elimination of the U.S. balance-of-payments
deficit was logically a prerequisite for the implementation of any liquidity-creating plan. "The
attainment of better balance-of-payments equilibrium
among members" presupposed any creation of new reserve assets, the communiqué said. This meant that
the United States should be "almost in equilibrium,"
explained Dutch Finance Minister Anne Vondeling, who
presided over the meeting. The U.S. delegation failed
to insert a phrase in the final communiqué implying
that a new reserve-creating mechanism might be made
operational once the U.S. deficit had been substantially reduced, albeit not entirely eliminated. "We
stopped that one," Debre told reporters at the conclusion of the two-day meeting.

The French Finance Minister said he voted
against expansion of the reform talks and any further
work toward the actual creation of a new source of
liquidity inasmuch as the persistent U.S.-payments
deficit was "an important source of inflation outside
the United States." In a handwritten statement distributed to the press, he said that he could not accept the agreement's implied hypothesis that money-
creating machinery could be established before the
United States had been in external balance for a
lengthy period of time.

The real significance of The Hague conference
was the expansion of the liquidity discussions to include semi-industrial and less-developed countries as
well as the ten. When the talks were initiated in
1963, the prevailing idea was that the international
liquidity problem was germane only to those countries
participating in the GAB. The liquidity studies,
like GAB, were to be a project only of the advanced,
industrialized, Western economic powers whose currencies were most used in international business transactions. Reserve creation, should it come about,
was viewed as being essentially a sophisticated extension of the Group-of-Ten currency swap existing
for the benefit of eleven countries only. Additional
currencies were not needed to support a new reserve
unit, and additional countries were not welcome in
the monetary reform talks.

The architect of the first phase of U.S. international monetary policy, Robert V. Roosa, saw a
clear-cut distinction between the already existent
capital shortage of the less-developed countries and
the potential future shortfall of liquidity increments in the foreign-exchange holdings of the industrialized countries. The basis of his argument was
that since the majority of the less-developed countries cannot afford the luxury of further sizable
accumulations of monetary reserves, "few of these
countries could retain any liquidity except as minimum working capital balances and as a base to support borrowing." An additional factor was Roosa's
belief that the difficulties of achieving appropriate
arrangements for creating a new unit were too great
to have to carry the additional burden of being simultaneously responsible for a "rather crucial" set of
aid decisions. Although it was both desirable and
feasible to indirectly make the new asset available
to non-ten countries, such as through a special arrangement within the IMF, he believed that it would
not be practical to combine the machinery of liquidity creation to assure the continued growth of world
trade with that of economic aid.[8]

As soon as the course of policy was changed by
Treasury Secretary Fowler in mid-1965, U.S. attitudes
vis-à-vis the limited-group approach also changed.
Confronted by the conservative outlooks of the Common Market countries but desirous of an ample introduction of new reserve assets, the United States
quickly found noncontinental countries, with their
expansionary economic outlook, to be natural allies.
This convergence of interests introduced a basic
element in the U.S. approach: a two-phased reform
process. The first phase would be under the aegis
of the Group of Ten, who would agree on the basis
of a reform plan. The second phase, Fowler told the
IMF, would be "designed primarily to assure that the
basic interests of all members of the fund in new
arrangements for the future of the world monetary
system will be adequately and appropriately considered and represented before significant intergovern-
mental agreements for formal structural improvements
of the monetary system are concluded."[9] In any
event, discrimination against or exclusion of the
vastly more numerous nonindustrialized countries
could never have been a tasteful U.S. policy, owing
to such political factors as the country's "special
relationship" with Latin America.

Meanwhile, until July, 1966, the EEC contingent
in the Group of Ten remained stubbornly firm in their
belief that reserve creation was the business only
of the ten. The eventual decision by the Group of
Ten to expand the liquidity talks to include the
twenty IMF executive directors, who represented the
then one-hundred and seven members of the fund, was
a compromise by the Europeans. They had reconciled
themselves to the inevitable. The strong preference
of the six to make final decisions on the substance
and procedures of a reform plan within the Group of
Ten notwithstanding, the sheer number of the other
countries ultimately overwhelmed the somewhat untenable argument that ten countries could justifiably
determine the future of the monetary system. Now,
the non-ten countries would be given a voice in the
planning of its reform. But the size of the voice
remained an unanswered question.

The Europeans employed three basic reasons to
explain why the power to construct and operate a
liquidity-creating arrangement should be left to the
Group of Ten. The first argument stated that, for
technical reasons, only a limited number of strong
countries could in fact provide the backbone of any
new reserve asset. It was Blessing's view that only
a limited group should operate a liquidity-creating
plan since only those industrial countries were in a
position to back such a scheme with their own resources. However, as he said at the 1965 IMF annual
meeting: "This does not mean that other countries
are excluded later on from such deliberations nor
does it necessarily mean that newly created liquidity
would be distributed only to assist this limited
group." The 1966 report of the deputies put it this
way: "A reserve unit scheme would consist of a network of mutual financial obligations." However,
since no formal provisions existed for "ensuring
that countries which made use of their allocations
of units should reconstitute them within a given
period of time, these obligations could only be
undertaken by a coherent group of countries."

Secondly, there was the argument that the liquidity problem was to the large, industrial countries
what development financing was to the less-developed
countries. They were, in other words, two distinctly
different problems in the same way as were the economics of these two sets of countries. In 1965,
French Finance Minister Giscard noted that there

were "wide differences" between development-
financing issues and international liquidity questions. What was relevant in the former was not how
to improve "the mechanisms through which national
economies communicate, but to alter the natural
distribution of wealth and the effective transfers
of resources."

Thirdly, it was argued that since the ultimate
outcome of any agreed-upon reserve plan would be the
creation of international money, any real influence by
the less-developed countries would be biased toward assuring the creation of a maximum amount. This would
produce a clear and present danger of international
inflation. As one German economic official privately
expressed it, anyone who would speak before the IMF
and propose the creation of a new money would find
more than half of his audience shouting "yes" before
he finished his talk.

A good summary of the continental views on making international monetary reform universal was supplied by Marius Holtrop, then President of the Dutch
Central Bank. He argued, in 1965, first that the "responsibilities involved in the creation of new reserve
assets should be borne mainly by those countries which
are best able to shoulder the resulting burden," and,
secondly, that the new reserve assets should be administered by the fund in a separate account. Then
came his opinion that the purpose of deliberate
creation of liquidity "should not be to bring about
a transfer of real resources to the countries that
might, on the basis of some agreed formula, be the
beneficiary of such creation, whether they are industrialized or developing nations." The purpose of
reserve creation "should be the prevention of a general tendency toward deflationary internal policies
or restrictive practices."

To the discomfort of those members of the Group
of Ten opposed to the idea of a universally distributed reserve asset, i.e., the EEC countries, the
semi-developed and underdeveloped countries refused
to quietly accept a Group-of-Ten planning monopoly.
The classic indictment against the limited-group
approach was the stinging address delivered by the
late Harold Holt, then Australian Finance Minister,
at the 1965 IMF annual meeting. In it, he bluntly
rejected the right of a small and strictly limited
group to make decisions on international financial

matters vitally affecting, in substance, if not also
in form, the rest of the world. With undiluted
frankness, he continued:

> There is some evidence that policies
> on these matters will be evolved in
> the limited Group of Ten, and then
> presented in a virtually unamendable
> form to this institution for adoption,
> however unsuitable some of the provi-
> sions may appear to many of our mem-
> bers. I have no wish to be critical
> of the Group of Ten. . . . But I speak
> now as one of the more than 90 coun-
> tries who are not included in the
> membership of the ten. I must say
> that it would be quite unacceptable to
> us to be confronted with a fait ac-
> compli, giving us no reasonable oppor-
> tunities for expressing our views in
> a manner which permitted these views
> to make some impact.
>
>   The Group of Ten, whatever its
> voting strength, can in no sense
> claim to be fully representative of
> this world institution nor, I imagine,
> would it claim to be so. I merely
> state, and certainly have no wish to
> do so offensively, that the Group of
> Ten can claim no mandate to legislate
> for the rest of the world. The fund
> can lay substantial claims to being a
> democratic institution. . . . The
> Group of Ten, on the other hand, is in
> no sense a representative group. . . .
> The question which faces us on this
> matter is, I am convinced, a critical
> one for the future of this organiza-
> tion. I see it as not merely a matter
> of resolving policies pertaining to
> these questions of liquidity, impor-
> tant though that may be. If the prec-
> edent becomes established that this
> is the way in which fundamental issues
> of international economic policy are
> to be resolved, then the value of these
> worldwide institutions will be under-
> mined, and their importance gravely
> diminished.[10]

When asked about the Group of Ten's decision to
expand the liquidity talks to include representation
of the rest of the free world, a good number of U.S.
Government and fund officials still refer to this
speech. The Australian's "tell-it-like-it-is"
message had hit home.

The speech by Holt's successor made one year
later displayed little mellowing in tone:

> I strongly oppose the idea of discrimi-
> nation within the world financial in-
> stitutions: No group of countries can
> assume an exclusive right to predeter-
> mine, outside the fund, matters vital
> to the interests of all fund members.
> Frequently I have asked myself what
> characteristic distinguishes this par-
> ticular group from the other fund
> members--apart from the fact that each
> country represented in the group is
> in the Northern Hemisphere. I have
> not yet found a persuasive answer
> other than that they were originally
> regarded as the major creditor coun-
> tries because of their participation
> in borrowing arrangements with the
> fund. But we all know how quickly
> international positions can change:
> the creditor of today is often the
> debtor of tomorrow.[11]

Having held a week-long conference before the
1965 IMF meeting, the twenty-nation Latin American
block (which includes the Philippines) selected Ar-
gentina to present its collective views on monetary
reform planning before the fund. The Argentine delegate noted that he thought the IMF organization constituted "the most appropriate forum for debating
this important question because of its open and multilateral nature." He went on to emphasize that "the
direction given to reforms of the monetary system,
and the setting up of bases to measure the adequacy
of the extent and the distribution of international
liquidity," were matters of "immediate concern" to
the Latin Americans.

The Executive Director of the fund, Pierre-Paul
Schweitzer, was also reluctant to allow the Group of
Ten to keep the question of liquidity creation among

themselves. Speaking before his organization's 1964 meeting, he said that an international organization provides the forum for "a balanced consideration, and hence the best reconciliation, of the various objectives in the international financial field as they affect all countries." One year later, he crisply decreed that "international liquidity is the business of the fund." At his direction, the staff of the IMF began its own independent study of reserve creation, the results of which were published as parts of the 1965 and 1966 annual reports of the fund. Consequently, throughout this period, there had been two separate but parallel studies in progress. Designed to focus on the liquidity problems of the developing countries, two other studies were issued by international organizations: one by the U.N. Conference on Trade and Development, the other by the Inter-American Committee on the Alliance for Progress. However, they were never formally considered by the Group of Ten.

The question of who would make the decisions on the nature, distribution, and use of the new international reserve asset strikes at the very political heart of the monetary reform exercise. Where to create the new asset and to administer it seems to be an innocuous institutional question, but it involves sensitive political issues. The European surplus countries were determined to influence national policies in debtor countries, particularly the United States, and to influence decisions on liquidity creation. Understandably, they looked askance at the possibility of losing an opportunity to impose strict discipline on these countries. They preferred to keep their hands firmly on the purse strings of international liquidity. The smaller the governing body, the greater would be the EEC countries' influence and power. A large, "public" forum such as the fund would not have been conducive to a maximization of continental values.

Since there was no genuinely technical need for the less-developed countries to participate, the EEC members of the Group of Ten were doubly determined to avoid the broad-based IMF and use the more intimate and less formal club of the ten. In the first place, the IMF gives a heavy predominance of voting rights to the United States and the United Kingdom (at that time, about 35 percent). When added to the voting power of the overwhelming majority of the

rest of the fund members who shared the liberal monetary orientation of the Anglo-Saxons, an IMF debate
could outflank and outvote the over-all power of
the EEC. The latter was also afraid that, given the
chance, the underdeveloped world would attempt to
convert the liquidity-creating exercise into an "aid
bonanza," over and above its control.

The European desire to deny a direct voice to
the non-ten countries was overwhelmed by three
factors. In the first place, most if not all of the
Common Market countries have direct political and
economic interests throughout Asia, Africa, and, to
a lesser extent, in Latin America. With the increasingly vociferous demands by the countries of
these continents for the right of representation in
a matter truly affecting the whole international
economy, it was unlikely that the Group of Ten could
have maintained a deaf ear indefinitely. If a reform plan had been quickly agreed upon, this situation may have been avoided. The Group of Ten might
have presented the world with a fait accompli in
early 1964 before universal interest in monetary reform had developed. But as one official said, it
became evident that the longer the ten talked, the
more it became necessary to pay attention to the
rest of the world. The pressure of mounting world
public opinion simply could not be ignored.

Secondly, there was the continuing pressure of
the "liberal" half of the Group of Ten, led by the
United States, who preferred a worldwide forum. The
preference for a universal approach by these countries was based on more than a genuine feeling that
all of the members of the IMF should have representation in the planning process and full participation
once the plan became operational. It was reasoned
that the larger the deliberating body, the more
liberal the new reserve asset which would be agreed
upon was likely to be.

The Common Market countries were unique not
only in their conservative outlook on future requirements for liquidity. They were also unique in their
fears of international inflation and their high preference for gold, both as a reserve instrument and
as an anchor for the new asset. In a debate with
universal participation, the power and influence of
the EEC would inevitably be more diluted than it
would be within the smaller Group of Ten. A simple

majority vote in the IMF theoretically could approve
a reform plan within that body. The other ninety-
odd members would logically support the liberal in
the Group of Ten, not the conservative--and in one
case reactionary--liquidity views held by the countries of the EEC. Understandably, Treasury Secretary
Fowler opposed with unrelenting pressure the conti-
nentals' limited-group approach from the time of his
conversion to the reform cause. He threatened more
than once to bypass the Group of Ten and introduce
the issue directly in the fund.

The third factor working against the continental approach was the technical problem of who would
administer the new asset, once activated, if only ten
nations were full participants. Although the fund
was the logical choice to administer a new international asset, any approach to its managing director
that it set up a special affiliate to manage a new
reserve asset for only a limited number of its members would have evoked strong overtones of prejudice
and privilege. Therefore, it would probably have
been rejected by the fund.

In addition, the Group of Ten, even if augmented
by such countries as Austria, Denmark, and Australia,
would not have the voting power necessaary to amend
the fund's Articles of Agreement to establish a new
fund operation. Amendments require three fifths of
the members who simultaneously have 80 percent of
the weighted voting power.

The realization that the rest of the IMF would
have to share in the distribution of any new reserve
asset had crept into the thinking of the Group of Ten
in advance of The Hague conference. In the early
part of 1966, the group began to talk in terms of
having any new plan distribute, albeit on a discrimi-
natory basis, the new asset to all fund members. The
deputies' report of 1966 noted that the advocates of
a limited group felt that the reserve needs of non-
group countries could be met either by creating repayable special drawing rights for them in the IMF
or by distributing units to them on a limited basis.
Nevertheless, lest liquidity be confused with foreign aid, the deputies again agreed that "deliberate-
reserve creation is not intended to effect permanent
transfers of real resources from such countries to
others."

The non-ten members of the fund had come full
circle. At the start of the liquidity talks, it
was felt that whatever the new means of reserve
creation, it should be administered only by those
countries that would have to provide the financial
backing to assure acceptability. As the talks
dragged on, Anglo-Saxon pressure within the ten and
the less-developed countries' pressure from without,
reinforced the growing realization that it would be
politically impossible to limit the privileges of
creating and receiving the new reserve assets to a
self-styled elite minority. A brief fling with the
notion that non-ten countries could be treated
separately and almost equally also had to be discarded as politically unworkable.

All IMF members were finally given the more
desirable status at The Hague of full participants
in both the negotiation and operation of the international monetary reform plan. This would have
immediate effects on the course of the talks. Distribution and use of the new asset had to reflect
the scarcity of gold in the less-developed countries,
yet activation of the plan and distribution of assets
still had to reflect a united EEC demand that the
six have veto power over these two critical areas.
The economic concept of monetary reform as an ad-
vanced-currency swap was discarded. But the larger
political concept of a resurgent Western Europe determined to end U.S. hegemony and share in the control of international liquidity was unchanged.

THE DEPUTIES' REPORT OF JULY, 1966

During The Hague meeting, the ministers and
governors also considered two reports which one
year previously they had requested be submitted to
them. To initiate the first phase of the desired
contingency planning, the ministers and governors,
at their September, 1965, meeting, had instructed
their deputies to resume "on an intensified basis"
their 1964 discussions. They were then to report
back "what basis of agreement can be reached on
improvements needed in the international monetary
system, including arrangements for the future creation of reserve assets, as and when needed, so as to
permit adequate provision for the reserve needs of

the world economy." The deputies were to report to
the ministers in the spring of 1966 on the progress
of their deliberations and on the scope of agreement
that they had found. The active participation of
the IMF, the OECD, the BIS, and Switzerland was also
welcomed. The ministers also expressed a desire to
have the report of the OECD's Working Party Three on
the balance-of-payments adjustment process submitted
simultaneously with the deputies' report.

There was no mistaking the fact that the real
decisions on international monetary reform would continue to emanate exclusively from the Group of Ten.
But the press release did conclude with recognition
that: "As soon as a basis for agreement on essential
points had been reached, it will be necessary to
proceed from this first phase to a broader consideration of the questions that affect the world economy
as a whole." Accordingly, the deputies were instructed to work out the details of "preparing for the
final enactment of any new arrangements at an appropriate forum for international discussions."

The report of the deputies examined the extent
of the consensus which existed first with respect to
the general improvement of the monetary system and
secondly with respect to deliberate-reserve creation.
For the third summer in a row, the financial leaders
of the Group of Ten had been presented with a study
of the international monetary situation.

The deputies had duly noted that all members
would not "proceed in the same way as regards all
technical details." Yet they agreed that any contingency plan should encompass the following basic
principles and elements:

> The fundamental purposes of reverse
> creation--Deliberate reserve crea-
> tion should not be directed to the
> financing of individual balance-of-
> payments deficits but should be
> based on a collective judgment of
> the reserve needs of the world as a
> whole. Reserves should be created
> (1) on a long-term basis to meet
> probable needs over a three-to-
> five year period ahead with provi-
> sion for adjustment in the light
> of circumstances, and (2) in amounts

sufficient to assure the growth in
reserves needed to avoid worldwide
deflationary pressures, disruptive
internal policies, or excess strain
on the monetary system, but not so
large as to create inflationary
pressure or to undermine payments
discipline and the general stability
of the system.

The basic characteristic of new
reserve assets--Supplementary reserve
assets should be unconditional in
principle; nevertheless, there must
be arrangements to prevent misuse of
the new assets and to prevent such
assets from being used simply to
change the composition of a country's
reserves. The new reserve unit should
be directly transferable between
monetary authorities and/or through
special reserve drawing rights in the
IMF. Both kinds of asset would origi-
nate in an automatic giving and
receiving of credit. Either would
confer the right to obtain other
participants' currencies.

The formula for distribution of
reserves--Deliberately created reserves
should be distributed on the basis of
IMF quotas plus GAB commitments or of
a formula similar to the one on which
the present IMF quotas are based.

Organizational arrangements--Provi-
sions for decisions on the creation
and management of deliberately created
reserve assets should reflect both
(1) the legitimate interest of all
countries in the adequacy of international reserves, and (2) the particular responsibilites of a limited
group of industrial countries.

The procedure for activation--Activa-
tion of a contingency plan should
take place when it was decided,
on the basis of collective judgment, that a clear need for reserves
would arise in the near future.[12]

The deputies also maintained agreement on the
same thesis which guided them in their 1963-64 study.
While global reserves continued to be sufficient for
present needs, "the existing sources of reserves are
unlikely to provide an adequate basis for world trade
and payments in the longer run, because a continuance
of large U.S. deficits must be ruled out as a source
of future reserve increases for the rest of the world,
and because gold alone is not likely to supply sufficient additions to monetary reserves."[13]

At first glance, the report represented a major
breakthrough in reaching a consensus on a reform plan.
The deputies second study did indeed culminate in a
number of significant agreements on technical issues.
But there was little or no progress toward attainment of a political consensus. Those technical
agreements that were reached were among a group of
nine, not among the Group of Ten. Although never
mentioned by name, France disassociated itself with
the substance of virtually the entire report. The
introduction set the tone: "One member indeed expressed the view that, in the present imbalance of
world payments, it would be inadvisable to formulate
a complete and detailed plan which could be adopted
in case a shortage of reserves should occur; this
member, therefore, felt unable to participate in the
discussion of the technical aspects of reserve creation."

Reflecting the French intransigence as well as
the absence of agreement on details among the rest
of the participants, the paper is replete with such
phrases as "we have not, at the present stage, gone
into this question in more detail," "most of us,"
and "those who favor." Three years of work and three
written reports notwithstanding, the 1966 deputies'
report graphically showed that unanimity on international monetary reform was still a long way from
fruition.

On the important issue of contingency planning,
for example, the report said that, while most members
considered that precise moment for the activation of
reserve creation was not then clearly discernible,
it still would be "prudent to establish a contingency
plan now." However, there apparently was complete
agreement that "there is no global shortage of reserves at the present time and that no immediate
action to create reserves is called for." The

deputies were therefore careful to draw a distinction "between planning for the contingency that most
of us visualize and activating, at a later stage, any
systematic procedure for deliberate-reserve creation."

One participant refused to accept even the principle of contingency planning, which he felt "would
at present time be inadvisable and even risky." This
was so because the final drafting of any reform plan
"would give rise to an irresistible temptation to
activate the agreement prematurely," i.e., before a
real need for additional reserves arose. The participant also noted that the monetary system's difficulties were due not to the likelihood of a shortage
of reserves in the near future but to the persistent
imbalances of the reserve-currency countries.

This lone dissenter was France. It adamantly
refused to encourage the developmemt of a new asset
in any way, shape, or form. No matter how removed
from actual implementation, additional reserves might
potentially aid and abet the financing of undesirable
U.S. foreign political-economic policies and negate
the pressure for their elimination already being
exerted by gold losses. Active efforts to eliminate
balance-of-payments deficits, said the French delegation, could be compromised if the problem of reserve creation were given precedence over "more
necessary" reforms; "in particular their action in
this field would be hampered by the presumed availability of new financing facilities. Far from helping to reinforce confidence, then, contingency
planning at this stage might further delay necessary
adjustments and thus aggravate the insecurity and
instability of international payments."

In considering the size and composition of the
group of countries which would participate in a plan
creating new reserve assets, the deputies wrote that
any arrangements had to "conform to two important
realities: first, that the aim of deliberate-reserve
creation is to meet the reserve needs of the world
as a whole; and, second, that a particular responsibility for the successful working of any scheme
must in practice rest on the major countries with a
key role in the functioning of the international
monetary system." There was also a brief mention of
the dual approach of the United States which would
provide reserve units primarily for the Group of Ten
and special fund drawing rights for all countries.

In the annex to their report, the deputies gave
a brief description of the five main schemes which
they had considered. The first of these, Scheme A,
was the updated version of the Emminger Plan, which
continued to reflect the views of Germany, Italy,
the Netherlands, and Belgium. The scheme would be
opened to all countries on a qualifying basis; the
bases for qualification included a convertible and
widely acceptable currency and assumption of the
obligations of multilateral economic surveillance.
The asset to be created under this plan would take
the form of a reserve unit with an absolute gold-
value guarantee. "A special feature of this scheme
is that, not only for ensuring acceptability, but
also for other reasons, each transfer of reserve
units would have to be accompanied, at least initially, by an equivalent transfer of gold; this obligation could be waived at the option of the country
receiving reserve units."

Scheme B was the U.S. proposal for the simultaneous creation of reserve units by a limited group
of countries and of Special Reserve Drawing Rights
(SRDR) to be created by and distributed to all members of the fund. SRDR's would be created for each
member country in the IMF in proportion to its quota
and would "be available at the discretion of the
holder on terms of use similar to those applying to
the gold tranche." The reserve units distributed to
a limited but open-ended group would have no link
with gold. "Their transferability and acceptability
would be assured by an initial holding limit for each
participant, together with a gold-value guarantee."

The third scheme was a loosely defined British
proposal. Reserve units with a gold guarantee would
be distributed to an open-ended group of countries;
they would be directly transferable among monetary
authorities. Each participant would have an upper-
and a lower-holding limit for these units. "Any
accumulation of units by an operating member above
his upper-holding limit would, at the member's option,
be convertible into gold by other operating members
who were below their upper-holding limits."

The final two proposals, schemes D and E, cor-
responded to the two alternative approaches previously suggested by the IMF. According to the first
proposal, of which there were a number of variants,
SRDR's would be established. They would consist of

unconditionally available quotas which would be made
automatically and immediately available to all fund
members.

The second IMF proposal in which all fund members could participate would be a reserve-unit
scheme to be administered by a specially created
affiliate of the Fund--the International Reserve
Fund (IRF). "Members participating in this exchange
would acquire claims on the IRF expressed in IRF
units of gold weight, and the IRF would acquire corresponding claims on the member. The exchange of
claims between the IRF and participants in the increases in question would be in amounts broadly
proportionate to IMF quotas."

COMMON MARKET UNITY AS A FACTOR

The twenty-fourth in a series of meetings held
by the EEC's finance ministers to informally discuss
financial matters of mutual concern met on September
12, 1966, in Luxembourg. The significance of this
particular meeting lay in the fact that it was
largely devoted to attempting for the first time to
formulate a common EEC strategy and position on
liquidity creation for use in the upcoming IMF- and
Group-of-Ten-ministerial meetings.

The communiqué issued after the Luxembourg meeting could not completely hide the fact that France
would not accede to the will of the majority. On the
basic question of whether or not to pursue contingency
planning, the rest of the EEC refused to waver; the
French still refused to accept the need for such
planning.

The text of the communiqué was couched in a
general but mostly positive tone. It stressed points
of agreement and glossed over points of disagreement
in an effort to convey a spirit of solidarity between
the six. "Without ignoring the divergences which
appear between them" in the Group of Ten, the communiqué said, the ministers and governors "confirmed
their agreement on the principles which inspired The
Hague communiqué of July 26." They noted their unity
on the following points:

1. Smooth operation of the international monetary system requires

elimination of serious and chronic
balance-of-payments imbalances. . . .

2. Despite differences of opinion as
to whether there should be contingency
planning for additional liquidity
creation, they consider that come what
may, such plans cannot be put into
effect before the main countries
have improved their balance of
payments, in particular reserve-
currency countries, or before collective noting of widespread reserve
shortage. Such a shortage is not
in being at the moment.

3. In contingency planning for the
creation of additional reserves and
adoption of all relevant decisions,
the group of the main industrialized
countries, to which EEC countries
belong, has a special responsibility.

4. . . . The economic growth of developing countries needs specific
means such as investment aid and the
various types of technical and trade
policy cooperation. It cannot be
sought by creation of additional
liquidity.[14]

Despite Michel Debre's plea for a united front
to be presented at the fund's annual meeting, the
communiqué clearly revealed the EEC's failure to
reach a common position on the need to pursue contingency planning. Still, three clear elements of
a common community position were visible: the elimination of the reserve-currency countries' balance-of-
payments deficits to take precedence over liquidity
creation, the need to insure control of the Group of
Ten over the new liquidity plan, and the need to
keep clearly distinct the problems of international
liquidity and economic development.

Any lingering fears that France would abandon
the next series of liquidity talks were dispelled
by the reports on the meeting in Luxembourg carried
in Le Monde. Chosen as the official source of the
frequent French press leaks, this Paris newspaper
was able to "authoritatively" report that France

was not going to repeat its "empty-chair" policy
employed during its 1965-66 boycott of the EEC's
institutions. France would attend the upcoming
joint deputies'-fund meeting, but its presence would
be a silent one. A policy of "sealed lips" would
be maintained. Le Monde also reported that official
French sources interpreted the Luxembourg communiqué
as meaning that the six had adopted a common attitude on making the elimination of the U.S.-payments
deficit into a firm precondition for any creation
of new international liquidity.

The Luxembourg meeting was to be a prelude to
additional meetings of both the EEC finance ministers and the EEC's Monetary Committee whose purpose would be to set the basis for a united position
on monetary reform in the larger Group-of-Ten forum.
Although no formal commitment ever existed to vote
identically in the IMF, the Common Market countries
feel a de facto commitment to consult among themselves on any question of substance, be it within
or outside of the community structure. The intense
political struggle that was the international monetary reform exercise reinforced the six's belief that
the existence of the partnership commitments inherent in the Treaty of Rome required internal discussions of any issue which might be inconsistent with
those commitments, i.e., with the interest of the
community. If one (or more) member country should
cast its vote against the community position in an
international forum, it would be symptomatic of a
community in disarray. For six countries obliged
by treaty to work so closely in harmony together
in the economic sector, the possibility of a public
split in either the Group of Ten or the fund was
anathema. Although France was not alone in opting
for a unified community posture on international
liquidity, it was the maverick French position which
most benefited from the resulting search for an accommodation of views and for unity. The search
essentially involved a reconcilement of France's
position with that held by the other five EEC
countries.

THE FIRST JOINT MEETING OF THE DEPUTIES
AND THE FUND, NOVEMBER, 1966

The first of four joint meetings between the
deputies of the Group of Ten and the executive

directors of the IMF was held November 28-30, 1966, at the fund's headquarters in Washington, D.C.   It was a large meeting, with more than sixty officials participating, and included ten deputies and alternates, all twenty executive directors and their alternates, plus representatives of the Swiss National Bank, the OECD, and the BIS.

Protocol problems were eliminated by having this and all the subsequent joint meetings designated as completely informal meetings of individuals.   It was not a meeting of the board of executive directors with the Group of Ten but a meeting between the individuals of these two groups.   Chairmanship of the meetings alternated between the fund's Managing Director, Schweitzer, and the deputies' Chairman, Otmar Emminger.

The four joint sessions were designated to allow the two groups which had performed the major studies of liquidity problems to meet together, to get acquainted, and to exchange views.   Informality was stressed to stimulate a "very full and frank exchange of views."   The IMF's 1966 annual report and the deputies' report of July, 1966, served as the starting points for the discussions; all participants were free to explain personal positions and views on all subjects covered in those two reports. Schweitzer explained that the first business of the joint meetings was "to cover the whole field of the problems which are presently open, to understand better the views of all the participants, and to try to ascertain what are the general lines of consensus and which are the major points on which some further exploration is needed."   As an informal meeting of individuals, no votes would or could even be taken.   The five-point agenda of the first joint meeting covered all the fundamental issues of deliberate reserve creation:

1.   The aims and objectives of reserve creation.

2.   The nature and form of deliberately created reserves, including their financing.

3.   Distribution of deliberately created reserves.

4. Utilization of new reserve
assets, including conditions for
the transfer of new reserve assets
and for assuring the acceptance
of these assets.

5. Conditions and circumstances
of activation of a contingency
plan.

In the press conference following the first
meeting, the fund's managing director declared that
the way the meeting proceeded "exceeded our most
hopeful expectations in the way of creating really
a unanimous desire to exchange views very frankly,
to understand the views of each participant, and to
find a common ground." The fear that the deputies
and the fund, "having worked separately, might re-
cite views at which their group had arrived and
which would impede the formation of a general opinion
where the views on the two groups were apart," proved
groundless. The meeting proved that there was
"really a common ground of understanding and cooperation between them."

The emphasis on the harmony which prevailed at
the first joint meeting was not simply polite, diplomatic rhetoric. The meeting was surprisingly successful in dispelling the misconceptions which the
deputies had of the fund's executive directors representing Asian, African, and Latin American countries, and vice versa. After each side had felt
the other out, it quickly became obvious that the
expected rancor and polemics would not in fact
materialize. Instead, there was to be an unexpectedly smooth meeting of the minds.

Each side found itself impressed and anxious to
work with the other. The deputies found the executive directors to be far more informed, reasonable,
serious, and conservative than they had expected.
Beforehand, they expected to do verbal battle with
a group of radicals whose main interest would be in
producing the maximum amount of new liquidity on the
most lenient terms possible. The executive directors, for their part, were expecting but did not
find an inward-looking rich man's club, oblivious
to the monetary needs of the rest of the world.
With a minimum of effort, an unhoped for atmosphere

of cordiality and mutual respect developed. Both
sides could move immediately to establish basic
areas of consensus.

During the first joint meeting, consensus was
reached on three major points. The first was that
any future deliberate-reserve creation "would be on
the basis of universality in the sense that distribution of any such newly created reserves would be
made to all the member countries of the fund according to a generally objective formula of the fund."
Significantly, the non-ten countries had attained
their objective of assuring the universality of any
monetary reform plan. Although they were obviously
not powerful enough to dictate the details of a new
reserve asset, the non-ten countries had received
assurance that the same formula for distribution and
use would apply equally to all countries. No distinction was to be made between countries inside or
outside the Group of Ten.

The second area of agreement stipulated that
creation of reserves "should meet global needs and
not the balance-of-payments needs of any individual
country." Finally, it was agreed that new reserves
should not be introduced as an "anticyclical way of
influencing the general economic situation of the
world."

Substantial progress toward consensus was made
at the initial meeting, but such crucial questions
as the conditions and the circumstances under which
a contingency plan should be activated, the rules
for decisionmaking, and whether there was to be any
transfer ratio-link between gold and the new asset
remained unresolved. Still, the newest series of
monetary talks had gotten off to an unexpectedly
sound start and would serve as a foundation for a
new, more advanced phase of negotiations.

There was only one major discordant note to mar
the noticeable harmony of the first joint meeting.
It was sounded by France. Coming at the zenith of
that country's gold offensive, a strong statement
was voiced by the French Director of the Treasury,
Maurice Perouse, which demanded that the joint
meetings study the future role of gold in the international monetary system.

To assure maximum play for France's lone, dissident voice, the substance of Perouse's statement

was leaked to the press in advance of its delivery.
Perouse insisted that the creation of a new reserve
asset could not be justified unless it had been
established beyond doubt that it were needed: "or
rather if, after the need had been established, it
did not seem possible to meet it in other ways," such
as an increase in the price of gold.

The first French priority was to have the question of the price of gold placed on the agenda of
the discussions. Because of an allegedly U.S.-
inspired ban on the discussion of the gold price
within the liquidity talks, it was an issue which
had not been sufficiently studied in depth. This
was an unacceptable situation. Perouse told the
meeting that "one should not exclude a priori any of
the methods suitable for increasing reserves if it
is believed that these reserves are not sufficient."

The French representative then added a new
wrinkle to his country's demand that heretofore
"taboo" topics be actively discussed in the liquidity talks. Perouse argued that the practice of
multilateral surveillance of balance-of-payments
related policies be extended to cover the conditions
under which reserve currencies are issued, held, and
circulated. The French believed that the OECD should
discuss not only the U.S. deficits but also the rate
of interest fixed "at the discretion of the U.S.
Treasury Department" on official foreign holdings of
U.S. Government securities. Since a reason repeatedly cited by foreign central banks for maintaining
their reserves in dollars rather than gold was this
interest rate, the French felt that this was a question concerning all countries.

This new demand by France was explained in
Le Monde as being a manifestation of the awkward
position which that country had placed itself in
at The Hague. It was there that France had agreed
to take part in further talks for the development
of a reform plan despite its affirmation that such
talks were useless, if not actually dangerous.
"Isn't one way of getting out of this contradiction
to bring up for discussion subjects which the adversary (in this case the United States) would at all
costs like to side-track?"

Perouse concluded by stating that France was
prepared to contribute actively to the present conversations only on the condition that they seriously

examined the complete range of international monetary problems, "without any taboo and in all objec-
tivity--which is what our role of experts imposes
on us."

The French effort to introduce the price of gold
as a topic for the agenda of the first joint meeting
was an apparent failure. In the post-meeting press
conference, Schweitzer said: "The price of gold was
not on the agenda of this meeting and will not be on
the agenda of any subsequent meeting. . . . I think
it is not even in the terms of reference of the
Group of Ten."

THE EUROPEAN ECONOMIC COMMUNITY FINANCE MINISTERS' MEETING, JANUARY, 1967

The next significant development in the monetary reform negotiations materialized at the January
16-17 meeting of the EEC finance ministers and central bank governors at The Hague. It was here that
the French made a strategic retreat from their policy of outright hostility to and harrassment of a
continued search for a new reserve asset. Facing
almost universal oppostion, the French dropped their
uncompromising insistence that an increase in the
price of gold be actively considered as a means of
supplementing existing international liquidity.

The French policy had not only failed to elicit
the slightest hint of support elsewhere, but its im-
practicality antagonized the rest of the EEC, as
well as the rest of the fund's member countries (with
the sole exception of gold-producing South Africa).
The French conceded their gold position, but not
without obtaining concessions from their EEC partners.

At The Hague, the French were instrumental in
authoring a unified Common Market position that the
problem of international liquidity could be handled
through an over-all reform of the IMF. The ministers
and governors, at France's bidding, announced that
they had decided, "while pursuing the examination
of the plans discussed hitherto, to instruct their
experts in the Monetary Committee of the European
Economic Community to study the improvement of the
methods of international credit without delay."

The French had effectively reopened the whole argument about unit schemes as opposed to additional drawing rights in the IMF. The general tone of thinking within the Group of Ten, exclusive of France, had moved distinctly in the direction of creating a full-scale reserve unit. This was the method explicitly mentioned by the Americans, Germans, Italians, Dutch, and British in late 1966. But now the Europeans were resurrecting the long-discarded U.S. advocacy of improving the monetary system through the strengthening and expansion of existing international credit institutions.

After the January meeting at The Hague, the liquidity talks could no longer focus exclusively on the creation of a new international currency unit. France had shifted its tactics, but its long-term strategy was clearly unchanged. It would still attempt to delay and divert the progression of the talks away from the direction of approving a liberal monetary reform plan. Although it could not do this alone--such a policy having already failed--it now had the tacit assistance of the EEC countries. The French position had been greatly strengthened.

Finance Minister Debre now hoped to press a revision of the voting procedures for quota changes and other business in the IMF in order to give the six a blocking vote when voting as a unit. His reform plan would be the absorption of the independent status of the GAB into a reformed fund structure as well as new arrangements for special but repayable drawing rights.

At a press conference after the meeting, Jelle Zijlstra, the Dutch Prime Minister and Finance Minister, told newsmen that the structure and functioning of the fund date from 1945 and "it is normal that this study would lead us to propose an adjustment, particularly as regards the quota in the fund and the voting system. This study will also lead to an examination as to how the European Economic Community will function in a reformed IMF, in the field of monetary policy." Zijlstra also stated that the six were now in full agreement that the question of the price of gold was "not typical." Despite the insistence of the Italian Treasury Minister, this judgment was not written into the final communiqué.

The EEC ministers' meeting once again demonstrated the centrifugal force exerted by France on
its partners. As the price for bowing to the will
of the majority and agreeing to negotiate a new
reserve asset, France had shifted the emphasis of
the countries possessing the balance of international monetary power away from reserve units and
into the direction of conventional credit expansion.

THE SECOND JOINT MEETING OF THE DEPUTIES
AND THE FUND, JANUARY, 1967

The second joint meeting of the IMF's executive
directors and the deputies took place shortly after
this EEC meeting, in London, on January 25-26. "We
are still in the exploratory stage," the Meeting
Chairman Emminger later told newsmen. "We are not
negotiating, but rather exploring the whole subject
of reserve asset creation and what goes with it."

The agenda of the second joint meeting paid
"particular attention" to four issues. The first
of these dealt with the conditions under which a
contingency plan for reserve creation would eventually be put into effect. Secondly, there was the
issue of how such a system of reserve creation was
to be controlled and would make the necessary decisions. The meeting also discussed the relationship between the IMF and any newly created reserve
assets. Finally, there again was a discussion on
the conditions and circumstances which would govern
the need for additional reserves in the future.
Emminger reported afterward that "definite progress"
had been made on an important aspect of decisionmaking. "There was a general consensus that there
could not be a formal two-stage voting procedure,
or, as one member of our group has put it, there
should not and could not be a formal bicameral
voting system or voting procedure with two separate
bodies having to vote."

Differences which looked "irreconcilable" were
to be left for the last negotiating phase; the joint
meetings were more concerned with a positive search
for a "common viewpoint without negotiating." In
Emminger's view, this category included the all-
important question of whether the new reserve asset
would take the form of a drawing right or a reserve

unit. It had already been found in previous explorations, however, that the "differences between the
two are not very great and to some extent are purely
technical." Both units and drawing rights are essentially the right to draw other countries' currencies, i.e., a mutual exchange of rights and
obligations, he pointed out.

NOTES

1. Otmar Emminger, "The Gold Exchange Standard
and the Price of Gold," in Randall Hinshaw, ed.,
Monetary Reform and the Price of Gold: Alternative
Approaches (Baltimore: Johns Hopkins Press, 1967),
p. 101.

2. Raymond Aron, "Is the European Idea Dying?"
The Atlantic Community Quarterly, V (Spring, 1967),
38-39.

3. Stanley Hoffman, "Discord in Community," in
William O. Wilcox and H. Field Haviland, Jr., eds.
The Atlantic Community--Progress and Prospects (New
York: Frederick A. Praeger, 1963), p. 17.

4. "The President's Economic Report to Congress,
1966" (Washington, D.C.: U.S. Government Printing
Office, 1966), p. 159.

5. Ibid.

6. U.S. Treasury Department Transcript of Dr.
Otmar Emminger's Press Conference, Washington, D.C.,
April 22, 1968, pp. 7-8.

7. Group of Ten, "Communiqué of Ministers and
Governors and Report of Deputies," July, 1966, p. ii.

8. Robert V. Roosa and Fred Hirsch, "Reserves,
Reserve Currencies, and Vehicle Currencies: An Argu-
ment," Essays in International Finance, No. 54
(Princeton: Princeton University Press, 1966), p. 37.

9. "Address delivered by Michel Debre, French
Minister of the Economy and Finance before the
French Chamber of Commerce of Montreal on January
13, 1967," (New York: Press Release of the French
Embassy Press and Information Service), pp. 1-20.

10. International Monetary Fund, "Summary Proceedings," Twentieth Annual Meeting, 1965 (Washington, D.C.: The Fund, 1966), p. 79.

11. International Monetary Fund, "Summary Proceedings," Twenty-First Annual Meeting, 1966 (Washington, D.C.: The Fund, 1967), pp. 73-74.

12. Derived by the author from U.S. Treasury Department summary of the Communiqué of Ministers and Governors and Reports of Deputies, July, 1966, p. 18.

13. Group of Ten, Communiqué of Ministers and Governors and Report of Deputies, July, 1966.

14. Agence Internationale D'Information pour la Presse, Europe, Daily Bulletin No. 2503, September 13, 1966, p. 1.

CHAPTER **5** THE FINAL
PHASE OF
NEGOTIATIONS,
1967

When France formally agreed in April, 1967, to
fully participate in the liquidity talks, the political will to produce an agreement had materialized.
Two months later, a single reform proposal had been
drafted and was being used as the basis for reaching
a final agreement.

THE MEETING OF THE EUROPEAN ECONOMIC
COMMUNITY FINANCE MINISTERS, APRIL, 1967

The two-day meeting of the EEC finance ministers
which convened in Munich on April 17 was one of the
more significant turning points in the monetary reform exercise. In the background was the height of
the "great gold debate" in the United States. Treasury Secretary Fowler's threats of possible unilateral
actions in a mid-March speech to the American Bankers
Association had been followed in early April by almost
simultaneous statements from the two largest banks in
the United States, the Bank of America and the Chase
Manhattan Bank, advocating that the government seriously consider changing its gold policy. Should the
drain on U.S. reserves continue, the banks suggested
a halt to further automatic sales of gold to foreign
monetary authorities. A multitude of conflicting
arguments simultaneously appeared in the press, publicly debating the consequences of what had once been
a sacrosanct and immutable policy. The Munich meeting also followed by only a few weeks the pledge by
the Bundesbank that it would refrain from further conversions of its dollar balances into gold.

The "hard-fought and at times stormy meeting"
produced a nebulous text which noted that the finance

ministers and central bank governors all believed that
the Common Market countries should occupy a place in
international monetary organizations which was more
befitting to their financial responsibilities, their
growing economic solidarity, and the growth of their
trade. It was noted that this quest would inspire
these countries to find a common position in the present discussions on the reform of the monetary system
and to maintain close cooperation in the future in
order to be able to jointly safeguard their rightful
interests.

Under the "spirit of cooperation prevailing,"
agreement was reached on a number of important points,
as described in the communiqué of the meeting:

1. The fact that an insufficiency of international liquidity does not exist at the moment does not
rule out reflections on measures to be adopted should
there be future needs of additional reserves.

2. Any measure to create additional reserves or
matching alternative solutions must be conditional on
its being jointly noted that there is a general shortage, on a better operation of the adjustment process,
and on a better balance in international financial
transactions; it must not be based on certain countries' balance-of-payments needs; this rules out fa-
vorable treatment to the benefit of one country or
one group of countries.

3. The present weight of the six's influence
and their union within the EEC should, at all events,
ensure them sufficient influence in the IMF and in
the voting procedure.

4. In these circumstances, should there be a
recognized inadequacy of international liquidities,
it will in the future be possible to envisage the
creation, within the IMF, of conditional and unconditional drawing rights.

5. There should, for debtors who have used all
or part of their independent drawing rights constantly
and over a long period, be the obligation to make repayment, so as to compel them to reestablish their
previous position concerning their independent drawing
rights, at the end of a given period.

6. Drawing rights in the IMF cannot be directly
transferred. However, the question of the bilateral

voluntary transferability of new drawing rights, which
should in any case take place under IMF control and
which should not change the original drawer country's
reimbursement obligation, will have to be considered
further in considerable detail.[1]

The ultimate effect of the Munich meeting, along
with insuring full French participation in further
talks, was the determination that whatever new asset
was created would physically take the form of partially repayable drawing rights within the IMF. For all
intents and purposes, the concept of reserve units
comparable to a new international money was now nothing more than a futile hope of the liberal countries
within the ten. Once the Germans went on record as
embracing the French inclination for drawing rights,
the EEC's and ultimately the Group of Ten's final
position was no longer in any real doubt.

The Munich accord was essentially a Franco-
German agreement. As such, it was a classic example
of power politics in the EEC. In return for the
French promise to support further contingency planning and the concept of unconditional drawing rights,
the Germans agreed to shift their support from the
creation of reserve units to a new drawing right
facility within the fund. Most of the groundwork
for this compromise had been worked out in advance
of the Munich meeting, during private bilateral talks
between Michel Debre, the French Finance Minister,
and Karl Schiller and Franz Josef Strauss, the German
Economics and Finance ministers.

Munich was viewed instantly in the United States
and the United Kingdom as being a sellout by the
Germans. Had the world witnessed "the second Munich?"
The Economist lamented that Munich might have once
again become "a synonym for the unsuccessful appeas-
ment of unreason." However, the Germans felt it appropriate to seek a compromise based on IMF drawing
rights, since they, like probably everyone except the
United States, believed that there could be no scheme
that left out the French and split the Common Market.
In other words, a limited reform plan was deemed better than none at all.

It was the U.S. Treasury Department's view that
the reserve assets envisioned in the Munich communiqué were "far too restrictive" and represented a
backward step in the negotiations. The basis of the
U.S. opposition centered on what was alleged to be

the unnecessary concession by Germany to the French.
On the basis of his conversations with the Italians
and the Dutch, Treasury Under Secretary Frederick
Deming told representatives of the German newspaper
Die Welt that he had concluded that neither country
considered Munich to represent a step forward. It
was his feeling that they both would have preferred
to create a new reserve unit.

The U.S. policy of "divide and conquer" had
failed. A week earlier, Fowler had personally written to Schiller suggesting that Germany not commit
itself in the name of EEC unity to any illiberal,
French-oriented position. However, Franco-German
solidarity remained paramount, even over the dissent
of the Italians and the Dutch.

The final communiqué of the meeting represented
only the most cynical veneer of true solidarity, for
the Franco-German embrace had presented not only the
liberal half of the Group of Ten but also the Italians
and the Dutch with a fait accompli. The liquidity
recommendations of the latter two countries had been
made for them in advance of Munich by the Germans and
the French.

When the thorniest issues were discussed, it was
found that there was a sharp division of views. A
basic source of the disagreement stemmed from the
fact, as explained by the Italians, that the French
interpreted the EEC agreement reached at The Hague in
January, to consider possible improvements in international credit methods, as having dismissed the possibility of the creation of new reserve units. The
Italians were joined by the Dutch in disputing this
interpretation and also in the view that "possible
improvements" meant that only refinements of existing
credit facilities were to be considered.

Both the Italian and Dutch delegations had
pressed for creation of new reserve units, as opposed
to simple drawing rights in the fund. Grudgingly,
however, their opposition withered in the face of
their two stronger partners' solidarity. After the
meeting, Italian Treasury Minister Colombo detailed
the Italian position to the press. He stated that a
number of important issues and conditions were still
unresolved, and if future studies did not lead to an
agreement, everyone would be able to resume examination of the creation of reserve units, which, in fact,
was never formally given up.

     The French reaction to Munich was predictable.
Once again they had successfully attracted the more
liberal EEC countries--Germany, Italy, and the
Netherlands--into a more conservative position, by
capitalizing on the ideal of Common Market unity.
Once again they had accomplished this through relatively minor concessions involving nothing more than
abandonment of an untenable policy (their total opposition to contingency planning) which lacked the
support of any other country in the Group of Ten.

     To Debre, Munich represented an "accord of
solidarity" despite what he conceded were "serious
divergences." He added at a press conference after
the meeting: "We are strong if we are united." The
French Finance Minister also referred to the importance of the fact that the Common Market countries
had undertaken among themselves not to follow divergent positions during the course of the upcoming Group
of Ten-IMF negotiations. He explained that should
any difficulty arise, it was agreed that either the
experts or the finance ministers of the EEC countries
would meet. His words reinforced the fact that for
the French, EEC unity was of paramount importance.
After all, it provided them their greatest political
leverage vis-à-vis the United States.

     After the first day's meeting, Debre, ignoring
the fact that, at The Hague, the EEC ministers had
agreed to continue the study of proposals other than
his own, publicly scored the Italian and Dutch opposition. "With the Germans and the Belgians," he said,
"we are talking the same language. Two other countries, however, have gone back on the agreement
reached in The Hague last January."2

     The Germans, for the record, felt very satisfied
with the concessions they had wrung from the French
at Munich. Proceeding from the basic premise that it
would be politically impossible to submit successfully
a reform plan found unacceptable by the French to the
Bundestag for approval, the Germans considered themselves highly successful in bringing France to a compromise position. They argued that it was possible
to create adequate liquidity arrangements through
drawings from the IMF.

     That the Germans had once again performed a sat-
isfactory and successful role as mediators between
the conflicting French and U.S. points of view was
the subject of a talk given in New York City by

Emminger on April 21. He said that it was a "regret-
table misunderstanding" that most of the U.S. financial press had interpreted Munich as an attempt by
the Common Market to delay or thwart altogether agreement on international monetary reform. Emminger dismissed the idea that the French had won the Germans
over to an antireform position. On the contrary, the
Munich agreement represented a "fair compromise" between conflicting points of view. Both the French and
the Germans had made concessions.

The French had succeeded in getting an agreement
on the form of the new reserve asset to their liking.
The other nations gained France's agreement on the
need to press forward with a serious attempt to reach
an accord on a plan for monetary reform in the reasonably near future. The important thing, Emminger said,
was that there was agreement among the EEC countries.
Without such agreement, negotiations would be "very
difficult," for the reason that the Germans would be
willing to proceed only very cautiously in the absence
of the French. The plan that was agreed upon in Munich was a workable one that, if implemented, could
make a meaningful contribution to the expansion of
the world's financial resources. Emminger dubbed the
tactics of the Munich talks as an attempt on the part
of the three "go-ahead" countries--Germany, Italy, and
the Netherlands--to overcome French opposition to the
idea of monetary reform.

The Munich communiqué left unanswered such important technical questions as repayment terms, rules for
decisionmaking, and whether the new drawing rights
would be segregated from traditional fund resources
and maintained by a separate fund facility. German
Finance Minister Strauss pointed out that the communiqué represented "instructions" for the EEC delegations at the next joint deputies-fund meeting. What
remained unclear, however, was how the six's positions
were subsequently to be coordinated and indeed unified. Because the Munich communiqué was so imprecise,
no one knew for sure the exact nature and import of
the concessions extended to the French. Added to this
confusion was the anger generated seemingly everywhere
but in France, Germany, and in neutral Belgium.

Almost overshadowed by this in-fighting was the
EEC's unanimity on the need for certain technical and
institutional reforms in the fund. The recommendation
that IMF voting procedures be revised to permit the

six to exercise influence proportionate to their economic and financial weight was contained in a technical memorandum on international monetary reform
submitted at Munich to the ministers and governors
by the Monetary Committee.

Established by the Treaty of Rome to foster
monetary and financial stability and coordination in
the EEC, the Monetary Committee had been charged in
the January meeting at The Hague with the task of
devoting particular attention to the improvement of
international credit procedures while continuing to
investigate the projects previously under discussion.
At the same time, the resolution also took into account the request of France to reexamine the existing rules and practices of the IMF.

The Monetary Committee performed the same function for the EEC's finance ministers as the deputies
did for the Group of Ten (the members of the committee in general were identical with the deputies of the
EEC countries). Throughout 1967, the primary concern
of the Monetary Committee was international monetary
problems. The responsibility for providing the technical data and advice on which to construct common
community positions on liquidity creation and on the
reform of the IMF had fallen on its shoulders.

On April 11, the final text of the French-domi-
nated report on reforming the IMF was approved by the
panel responsible for its drafting. The report presented to the EEC ministers was extremely technical
and put forward various alternatives for the consideration of the ministers. Inherent in any emphasis on
extension of the fund's credit facilities as the means
of creating additional liquidity was a greater voice
in that organization for the EEC countries.

A very few important decisions in the IMF, quota
increases and amendments, for example, required an
80 percent majority of the weighted vote. Only the
United States, with approximately 22 percent of the
voting power, could unilaterally block, i.e., veto,
these types of proposals. If the fund were to become
the focal point for liquidity creation, the six would
not be content with anything less than similar veto
power. Accordingly, the Monetary Committee's report
suggested an increase of this special 80 percent majority figure to 85 percent. The Common Market countries, with about 16.5 percent of the total voting

power in the fund, would thus be assured of an effective veto over all important decisions related to
regular fund activities in general and the new reform
plan in particular.

Without discussing it in detail, the EEC ministers approved the report during the Munich meeting.
The ministers thereupon asked the Monetary Committee
to follow through on its various proposals for the
reform of the fund and to put them into a form in
which they could formally be presented to that organization.

THE THIRD AND FOURTH JOINT MEETINGS
OF THE DEPUTIES AND THE FUND

The third joint meeting of the deputies and the
fund executive directors took place for three days in
Washington, D.C., beginning on April 24. The Munich
accord and the Monetary Committee's report were in
the limelight during the working meetings. The six
maintained a united position throughout. Even the
Italian delegation, Le Monde happily reported, spoke
out in perfect conformity with the plan agreed upon
at Munich. After stating their basic position, hostile to the proposals of the EEC position, the United
States took on an attitude more questioning than
agressive, apparently in an effort to determine the
limits and possibilities of the still imprecisely
defined community position.

At the traditional post-meeting news conference,
Pierre-Paul Schweitzer said that the first of the two
major items on the agenda was a general discussion of
the possible qualitative and quantitative criteria to
assess the need for additional reserves and its urgency. The discussion had led only to the conclusion
that it would have to be decided as a matter of collective judgment.

The second item was consideration of the main
problems related to a scheme for deliberate-reserve
creation. Schweitzer said that, in discussing this
item, the participants had before them illustrative
schemes prepared by the fund staff, the main function
of which was "to present the various items and topics
that any scheme must deal with." Also utilized were
specific points submitted by various participants, as

well as the Munich communiqué, "the ideas of which were of course taken up by the participants representing these countries."

There were actually two sets of illustrative plans prepared between the second and third, and then again between the third and fourth joint meetings by the fund staff. The first of these described a reform scheme based on reserve units to be administered by a specially created fund affiliate. The second involved a new drawing-rights agreement which would be merged with existing fund resources. In a sense, automatic drawing rights would be grafted into existing fund quotas. By the spring of 1967, however, the main difference between the ideas of drawing rights and reserve units as formulated by the IMF was semantic.

The fund's Managing Director told the press that his staff would provide further studies on some of the points which were still unresolved in order to make available all elements for a judgment. Schweitzer remained optimistic that "the broad outlines of a plan" could be presented to the IMF's board of governors at the forthcoming annual meeting.

The major accomplishment of the last of the four joint meetings held in Paris, June 19-21, was the drafting of a basic "working document" containing the outline of a single reform plan based on an automatic drawing right within the framework of the IMF. After more than three and one-half years of discussion, the Group of Ten had reached the stage of consensus whereby the elements of a single plan could be assembled in one document that would be the basis for negotiation in future meetings at the ministerial level.

With the conclusion of the joint meetings, two ministerial meetings were planned for July: the first by the EEC's finance ministers and the second by the Group of Ten's Ministers and Governors. The task of the latter meeting was to resolve the remaining areas of disagreement in the outline agreement. The outline itself was replete with brackets containing the conflicting viewpoints on a number of important issues. Schweitzer explained that a number of "open questions" were inevitable in a working paper of the type being used. The unsettled issues, he added, "would call for decisions by ministers,

that is, decisions of a political nature. We as experts have done our best to bring these controversial
points out as clearly as possible and to put to ministers clear alternatives for their solution."

The basic question of drawing rights versus
reserve unit had now been all but irrevocably finalized. Although Emminger tactfully commented that
the concept of reserve units, while not "definitively
dead" was "half dead," the liberals in the Group of
Ten realistically reconciled themselves to new forms
of drawing rights in the IMF. What really remained
to be settled was whether the new asset would be more
in the direction of the creation of a full-scale
reserve or simply be an enlargement of existing
credit facilities. This would be determined by the
arithmetical question: to what extent repayment,
or reconstitution, of the drawings would be required.

The four joint meetings were subsequently derided in the press as being at best valuable for
their free exchange of ideas and at worst as being
nothing more than "teach-ins for the lesser nations."
The joint meetings did not alter the basic fact that
the important political decisions would have to be
made in the ministerial meetings of the Group of
Ten. When the latter made a firm decision, the fund
could be nothing more than a rubber stamp. Despite
this fact, the universal participation of these meetings materially affected the final form of the monetary reform agreement. In particular, the plan
probably would have been less universal in character,
at best giving only a limited participation of jun-
ior status to the non-ten countries. Secondly,
dropping the link with gold became inevitable with
the acceptance of a universal reserve creation plan.
It was impractical to insist on a gold link when
countries with very small gold holdings were to be
included in the plan.

The joint meetings also extended the opportunity
for the IMF's uniquely qualified staff of international civil servants to supplement the, efforts of
the Group of Ten's deputies. The fund staff was a
"neutral secretariat" which outdid itself in accom-
plishing something which the deputies never could:
the actual drafting on paper of an outline of a
single reform plan. The large and thoroughly experienced fund staff, unlike the deputies, could
work continuously together for extended periods of

time on the wording of specific provisions. They
also could advance a plan without its having the
connotation of being the work of a particular country. The IMF's expertise and pragmatism helped to
convert the liquidity talks from a repetition of
old arguments to a discussion of specifics.

THE JULY MEETING OF THE EUROPEAN
ECONOMIC COMMUNITY FINANCE MINISTERS

With a Group of Ten ministerial meeting scheduled to be held later in the month, the EEC finance
ministers and central bank governors, as was their
wont, held a dress rehearsal for their performance
in the larger group. Meeting in Brussels on July 4,
they once again failed to produce a genuine harmony
of policies, even though the liquidity talks were
moving into their final, climactic phase. As with
its predecessors at The Hague and Munich, the results
of this ministerial meeting seemed to have as many
interpretations as participants.

Of the ten points on the Brussels agenda concerning monetary reform, only three were dealt with
in detail. On the vital question of reconstitution,
the six were unable to agree on a single formula
despite protracted discussions. They could only
agree in principle that it would be desirable for
the stipulation of reconstitution to be included in
the text of the final agreement and that reconstitution should be in some way (provided that the appropriate formula were found) tied to the concept of the
amount and duration of credits requested.

The French had proposed that reimbursements
should start if more than 50 percent of a country's
quota were utilized over a period of four years, or,
alternatively, 33 percent over a six-year period.
Attached to the four-year proposal was the suggestion that a country which utilized its entire drawing-rights allocation would have to make reconstitution in but two years.

The most lenient formula, suggested by the
Dutch, would require some reimbursement only when a
country had used 100 percent of its drawing rights
over a five-year period. It was also the Dutch who
prevented adoption of an arithmetic formula defining

the criteria for reconstitution. The Dutch delegation successfully insisted that the rules of reimbursement should be left to the full meeting of the
Group of Ten. "If we have accepted the idea that
rules for reconstitution must be made, we think that
these should be discussed with the ten rather than the
six," Dutch Finance Minister Hendrikus Witteveen told
reporters. Asked Le Monde indignantly, "Does this
mean that Holland thinks, on a question of technique
such as this, that one of the six may express within
the Group of Ten a divergent point of view from its
EEC partners?" France's concern for unity in the
liquidity talks obviously transcended its official
delegation.

The Common Market countries also failed to
reach any definitive agreement on the exact procedure for establishing and administering the new
drawing facilities, i.e., whether or not a separate
fund account should be established for the purpose
of handling the new drawing rights separately from
normal IMF transactions.

As at Munich, however, there was a unified determination by the six to insist that the percentage
of votes needed to approve all major reform deci-
sions--especially the vote for activating the new
drawing rights--would be raised to 85 percent so
that a unified EEC could have effective veto power.

The official communiqué of the Brussels meeting
was firmly seconded by French and EEC commission
spokesmen. It boasted that further progress had
been made in reaching a common position on liquidity
creation. But in the background, the Dutch openly
and the Italians discreetly insisted that the major
points were still unresolved and would be acted on
only in the wider forum of the Group of Ten ministerial meeting scheduled to be held later that month.

THE UNITED STATES'
WOOING OF THE GERMANS

By 1968, the Germans clearly had emerged as not
only the ultimate mediator but also the ultimate
factor in the balance of power in the international
monetary reform talks. It was Germany's position
which would largely determine in whose favor the

final reform plan would lean: whether it would be
in the most liberal direction, as advocated by the
United States, or in the most conservative direction,
as preferred by the French.

France's channel of communication with the all-
important German decisionmakers was primarily the EEC
finance ministers' meetings. The U.S. channel, for
the most part not activated until the early spring of
1967, consisted of a number of bilateral contacts
with representatives of the German Economics Ministry. These meetings and letters, primarily with
Economics Minister Karl Schiller, culminated in a
meeting between President Johnson and Chancellor
Kurt Kiesinger in the middle of August. Although
defense matters were the focal point of their controversies, the balance-of-payments costs of the
U.S. troop commitment inevitably led to a discussion
of the prospects for international monetary reform.
The liquidity issue had once again intruded into
political discussions at the highest level.

The U.S. Treasury Department pressed three
major themes during these contacts. The first was
the familiar argument that to be unprepared for an
inevitable shortage of international liquidity would
eventually result in a trend toward restrictive and
deflationary economic policies by countries intent
on preserving their increasingly hard-to-come-by reserves.

Secondly, the United States continued to insist
that what had to be created was a first-class asset
that would, like the dollar, be good as gold. The
United States wanted an asset sufficiently attractive
to assure its inclusion by central banks in their
reserve statistics. In short, the United States
would not settle merely for a glamorous augmentation
of conventional credit facilities.

The third point of emphasis took the form of
U.S. advice to the Germans on how to deal with the
French. It was suggested that the future course of
the world's monetary system could not logically be
keyed to a single reluctant country. The best way
to make the French cooperative was not by compromise
but by demonstrated resolution and firmness on the
part of the more liberal Germans. Once convinced
that the rest of the community was fully prepared to
abandon the lone dissenter and join the rest of the

world in a liquidity-creating plan, the U.S. scenario had the French adopting a far more flexible and liberal policy.

This was also the basic rationale behind the continued U.S. opposition to the granting of a formal veto in the reform plan to the EEC when it voted as a bloc. If such a veto were granted, the United States foresaw the need for the rest of the Common Market countries to drag along a single "delinquent," thereby making it inevitable that the lowest common denominator of an agreement would have to be adopted.

The Germans, for their part, assured this country that they fully agreed it was necessary to reach final agreement on a plan, even though there was no existence or prospect of a liquidity shortage. When this situation finally presented itself, the Germans, like the United States, wanted to be in a position to act quickly. However, they felt that it was both possible and preferable to create new liquidity through the credit arrangements envisioned at Munich. The presence of some stipulation for repayment of the asset would do much to assuage continental fears of international inflationary pressures.

The Germans also insisted that the concept of a common EEC position on international monetary affairs was important, and agreement on a plan could not come about at the expense of that organization's unity. The possibility of summarily abandoning the French to a splendid isolation was totally unacceptable. No reform plan, they argued, was likely to be approved by the German Bundestag if it had been rejected by the French or drafted in their absence.

The Germans acknowledged but did not relish their role of mediators between the United States and France. They did feel, however, that there was still sufficient flexibility in the six's position on such matters as reconstitution and transferability to keep the Franco-American schism from being considered insurmountable. They emphasized that there was only one issue firmly resolved within the EEC: the need to be given an effective veto over such major decisions as the activation and quantitative allocation of the new reserve asset. In every other major area, there was still room for maneuverability and compromise. For Germany, the unhappy alternative to reconciling this gulf would be to

incur the intense displeasure of one or both of its
major allies.

THE LONDON MEETINGS OF THE
GROUP-OF-TEN MINISTERS,
JULY AND AUGUST

The fourth joint meeting of the deputies and
the IMF executive directors had produced a single
draft document containing the outline of a reserve-
creating plan based on a new system of drawing
rights. What had been presented by the fund staff
as a complete and tightly written paper was, however, "completely messed up" during that meeting.
The French and other national delegations at that
time had proceeded to insert a number of reserva-
tions and alternatives to the key points of the plan.
In terms of drafting, the paper which emerged was
a "God-awful mess."

The outline of the monetary reform plan was
riddled with brackets containing, as in the case of
the reconstitution formula, up to five alternative
proposals for still unresolved issues. At this
point, the technicians had exhausted their mandate.
The final elimination and reconciliation of the
bracketed passages would require a political decision by the ministers of the Group of Ten.

The climax of the international monetary reform
exercise was scheduled for July 18-19 in London. It
was hoped that here the Group of Ten finance ministers and central bank governors could make all of
those political decisions which were the requisites
for a final agreement.

The meeting opened with statements of over-all
position by the more important delegations and a
report by Dr. Emminger, Chairman of the deputies,
on the broad areas of agreement and the remaining
areas of disagreement. Two major areas of contention were present at the London meeting. The first
was the question of voting rules to assure, if the
six voted as a bloc, that no decisions on activation
or on the amount of allocation could be made over
their opposition, i.e., they would have veto power.
The EEC therefore pressed their insistence that a
majority of 85 percent be required for these

decisions. Fowler continued to voice U.S. opposition to such a move but offered a compromise. There would be a majority vote of 80 percent (precluding blocking power to the Common Market countries with their 16.5 percent vote) if the new drawing rights amounted to no more than $1 billion annually over the projected five-year period. However, if the drawing rights moved to the $2 billion annual figure preferred by the United States, the 85 percent vote would be installed.

The six were also united here in proposing that no country would be compelled to accept drawing rights from other countries in an amount more than twice its own allocation of drawing rights in the new scheme.

The second and most important question pertained to the reconstitution of the new drawings. The higher the percentage to be reconstituted, the less like money and more like credit would be the new reserve asset. In this instance, the confrontation was primarily one between the United States and France, not the United States and the Common Market.

The French proposal was that any country which used an average of more than 50 percent of its new drawing rights over a four-year period would have to reconstitute that portion. If the new asset were to be a credit, Debre suggested, there had to be a repayment provision. Secretary Fowler reportedly insisted that the new asset was supposed to be "as good as gold, a first-line asset, something the public believes in," and maintained that no agreement at all would be better than an inadequate scheme.

It was at this point that the Italians introduced as a compromise a variation of the old "harmonization" principle. Their suggestion required that participants use what were now being referred to as "special reserve drawings rights" at some fixed pace with their use of gold and foreign exchange holdings. In order to hold the proportion of drawing rights constant, after a certain lapse of time, a country would have to reestablish the same ratio existing between its drawing rights and its traditional reserves when the plan was initiated. Although neither side was overly enthused with the Italian suggestion, both France and the United States agreed to see what their deputies could make of the compromise. The meeting was then adjourned.

Nothing substantive was accomplished at the meeting, save the official and conclusive discarding of the unit concept in favor of the drawing-rights approach. Nothing conclusive could be agreed upon because apparently Debre had not yet been given the authority to make a final commitment. Still, the communiqué issued after the meeting emphasized the positive. The ministers and governors noted that they had "narrowed the remaining differences of view" among themselves and had given guidance to their deputies to work out in the coming weeks "proposals acceptable to all." They were optimistic that agreement would be reached on an outline plan to be embodied in a resolution at the forthcoming IMF annual meeting.

Two meetings of the deputies, one held immediately after the ministerial meeting and one at the end of July, failed to achieve any real breakthroughs. The deputies were prepared to successfully resolve technical problems but not political ones. And at this point, technical problems were few and far between.

Although the United States continued to talk a tough line, it was obvious that this country would have to yield on the first major unresolved question, veto power for the EEC bloc, and also would have to accept a partial reconstitution provision. Additionally, the United States by early August was, like the Europeans, talking in terms of annual drawing-rights allocations of $1 billion instead of $2 billion.

The growing optimism prevalent in early August might also be traced to a seemingly irrelevant gesture by Debre. When it became obvious that the first London meeting was not going to reach any conclusive agreement, the presiding chairman of the ministers, Callaghan of Great Britain, read off a list of prospective dates for a follow-up ministerial meeting. All were in August, traditionally a vacation month on the continent. Yet Debre had raised his hand for virtually every proposed date. By simply pleading inconvenience, he could have effectively delayed final agreement indefinitely.

As the second ministerial meeting approached, there was every confidence in its success. The essence of progress made at London, an unnamed U.S. official had said, "is the political will to come

up with a plan." Ideally, he declared, it would
have been fine if the ministers could have knocked
out all the brackets, meaning choosing between all
the alternatives. "But maybe they can do in late
August what we hoped to do in mid-July."[3]

This is exactly what the second London ministerial meeting accomplished. The meeting, which
lasted from 10:00 A.M. until nearly midnight on
August 26, was finally able to arrive at a reconstitution formula which both France and the United
States could live with. It was also able to secure
U.S. agreement for giving the EEC a blocking vote.
France had originally reintroduced its formula of
permitting a 50 percent average use over a four-year
period without repayment. The United States still
advocated the most minimal reconstitution requirement.

Ever the conciliators, the Germans, with support from the Italians, then proposed a compromise
figure of 75 percent. After much additional debate
and continued display of German-American-Italian
solidarity and determination, a 70 percent reconstitution was found to be acceptable to all parties.
To minimize political connotations, the Canadians
were called on to formally introduce the 70 percent
motion. The vote was taken, the measure passed
unanimously, the last real problem had been solved,
and the meeting was adjourned. Agreement had been
finally reached on the essentials of a contingency
monetary reform plan.

The resulting communiqué said:

> The ministers and governors agreed
> on the text of an outline of a con-
> tingency plan which they would be
> prepared to support at the forth-
> coming annual meeting of the gov-
> ernors of the IMF in Rio de Janeiro.
> This outline will now be considered
> by the executive directors of the
> fund. It is expected that the out-
> line as approved by them will be
> embodied in a resolution at the
> forthcoming annual meeting of the
> governors of the IMF in Rio de
> Janeiro.[4]

The ministers and governors also noted that they had concentrated their discussions on a number of key features of the plan on which differences had not been previously resolved. In particular they had agreed that:

> Decisions on the basic period for, timing of, and the amount and rate of allocation of the new drawing rights should be taken by the board of governors of the IMF by a majority of 85 percent of the total voting power. Members which use their new drawing rights would incur an obligation to reconstitute their position in accordance with principles which will take account of the amount and duration of the use.[5]

Reconstitution, it was noted, would apply to any participant to the extent that its net average use of the new facility over the five-year base period exceeded 70 percent of its total allocation.

The climax of the reform negotiations had been successful because the political will for a settlement had indeed existed. That the Group of Ten ministers and governors had returned to London to reach an agreement was sensed throughout the afternoon and evening of the meeting. After the meeting adjourned, Chairman Callaghan confided to members of the U.S. delegation that he had tightly and forcefully run the meeting as if he had had some real power. He realized that any of the participants could have gotten up and walked out anytime they wanted, but he kept a forceful rein on the meeting because he felt that all truly wanted to reach an agreement.

What was striking, beamed Le Monde, were the efforts in the Group of Ten made by the different ministers, be they French or American, to approach the international liquidity problem in a pragmatic and undogmatic manner. "This attitude is explained by the fact that, after all, France as well as the United States belongs to the same economic and financial system, and that despite their difference, the two countries have a basic interest in maintaining that system."

APPROVAL OF AN OUTLINE AGREEMENT,
SEPTEMBER, 1967

On September 9, the fund's twenty executive directors added their approval to the outline adopted at London by the Group of Ten. This was a routine step preliminary to the submission of the outline to the 107-nation board of governors at their 1967 annual meeting, scheduled to begin in Rio de Janeiro on September 25.

Two days later, the IMF published the full text of the outline agreement, which is reproduced in the Appendix. It bore the official title "Outline of a Facility Based on Special Drawing Rights in the Fund." The new facility was described in an introductory paragraph as being "intended to meet the need, as and when it arises, for a supplement to existing reserve assets." It would be established within the framework of the IMF and, therefore, by an amendment of the fund's Articles of Agreement.

The mechanics of the drawing-rights facility are explained in the nine sections of the six-page outline. In the first section, "Establishment of a Special Drawing Account in the Fund," it is stipulated that the IMF is to separate the operation of and resources available under the special-drawing account from regular fund transactions. This account administers all the operations relating to special drawing rights (SDR's). The traditional borrowing transactions in the fund continue to be operated by what is referred to as the general account.

Participation in the special drawing account is open to any IMF member country which undertakes the obligations of the amendment. Members' quotas for the special drawing accounts are proportionate to existing quotas in the general account (voting power is also proportionate to regular quotas).

The decision to activate the agreement includes a "basic period" during which SDR's will be allocated at specified intervals. This so-called basic period was set at five years. An 85 percent majority of the voting power of participants will be required for decisions on the basic period for, the timing of, and the amount and rate of allocation of SDR's.

This figure respects the EEC's 16.5 percent voting power.

SDR's will actually be used to acquire an equivalent amount of a convertible currency (primarily dollars). The country providing this currency receives as payment an equivalent dollar amount of SDR's. (Only one country, the United States, can turn figuratively to the printing press rather than to its foreign reserves when being credited with the SDR's of another country.) The drawing country will then use the hard currencies it has acquired to support the value of its own currency in the exchange market or to transfer the currencies outright to a creditor country. In all cases, a participating country is "expected to use its special drawing rights only for balance-of-payments needs or in the light of developments in its total reserves and not for the sole purpose of changing the composition of its reserves."

The user of SDR's thus will acquire currency, not out of fund-held resources but from the reserve holdings of other participants. Purchases of currencies are to be made from countries with strong balance-of-payments and reserve positions, in effect following the fund's existing rule of thumb for the selection of currencies to be used in its regular lending operations. Special provision is also made for a participant to use SDR's to purchase balances of its own currency held by another participant, provided the latter agrees. Hence, the United States could use SDR's to purchase unwanted dollars from potential gold buyers.

Every participating country is obliged to provide its currency in exchange for SDR's until its holdings of the new asset, including its original allocation, are equal to three times the amount of this original allocation. For example, a country whose initial allocation was equal to $100 million and who had used none of its SDR's would have a net-acceptance obligation of $200 million. If this same country had transferred all of its initial allocation to other countries, its net-acceptance obligation would be $300 million. Any country is free to accept and hold SDR's in an unlimited amount. To make it more desirable for surplus countries to do just this, SDR's are to carry a gold-value guarantee (this involves pegging their value to the official gold price and not to any national currency) and will pay a modest rate of interest to countries acquiring them from other countries.

As stipulated at the last London ministerial meeting of the Group of Ten, participating countries which extensively use their SDR allocation to finance large and persistent balance-of-payments deficits will incur an obligation to reconstitute their original allocation, depending on the exact amount and duration of this use. The reconstitution provision specifies that a participant's average use of SDR's over the five-year basic period is not to exceed 70 percent of its total average allocations for those years. When translated in terms of holdings, the obligation will require that over any five-year period a country's average daily holdings should be at least 30 percent of the average of its net cumulative allocations. Should a participant exceed a 70 percent average daily usage of its allocations during some part of the five-year period, it would then have to increase its holdings above the 30 percent level at the end of the basic period for a period long enough to assure that its maximum, average usage level were only 70 percent. Two years after the initial allocation, the IMF will begin making monthly calculations to ascertain the extent to which a participant heavily utilizing its SDR's might need to reacquire (with gold or convertible currencies) new SDR balances to fulfill the reconstitution obligation. It may be that this rather cumbersome requirement eventually will be abolished altogether, assuming participants in the plan with 85 percent of the voting power deem it to be more trouble than it is worth.

The dynamics of the monetary reform plan are illustrated in the following hypothetical example constructed by the IMF. Country A, with an SDR allocation of $10 million, has the need and desire to use one half of its drawing rights to finance a balance-of-payments deficit. It would first check with the IMF to ascertain to exactly which participant(s) it should transfer its rights in exchange for convertible currency.

The fund would at any given time maintain a list of participating countries whose balance-of-payments and reserve situations were considered satisfactory. From this list, it would designate one or more appropriate countries to provide currency

against SDR's. If, for example, Germany and Italy
were designated, the fund would notify these two
countries that it was crediting their holdings in
the special drawing account with the equivalent of
$2.5 million each. Germany and Italy would be re-
quested to provide Country A with a corresponding
amount of currency "convertible in fact." At the
same time, the fund would debit Country A's SDR
holdings by the equivalent of the $5 million in con-
vertible currencies which it could then spend. As
long as Country A used over a period of five years
an average of no more than 70 percent of its SDR
allocation, there would be no recognition obligation.

The outline was unceremoniously approved on
September 29, 1967, the last day of the Rio meeting.
Erik Brofoss, governor for Norway and chairman of
the meeting, simply declared Resolution No. 22-8
adopted when there was no objection from the floor
following a pro forma report of the Procedures Committee.

The resolution adopted called for the "establishment of a facility based on special drawing
rights in the fund and modifications in the rules
and practices of the fund." Accepted as part of
the monetary reform resolution was the EEC-inspired
call for a study of reform of the fund itself. The
resolution noted that whereas an outline agreement
had already been agreed upon and whereas studies
were currently under way on possible improvements
in the present rules and practices of the fund,
the board of governors resolved to have the executive directors do the following:

1. Proceed with their work relating to both
(a) the establishment in the fund of a new facility
on the basis of the outline, and (b) improvements
in the recent rules and practices of the fund based
on developments in world economic conditions and the
experience of the fund since the adoption of the
Articles of Agreement of the fund; and

2. Submit to the board of governors as soon as
possible but not later than March 31, 1968, (a) a
report proposing amendments to the Articles of Agreement and the By-Laws for the purpose of establishing a
new facility on the basis of the outline, and (b) a
report proposing such amendments to the Articles of
Agreement and the By-Laws as would be required to give
effect to those modifications in the present rules

and practices of the fund that the executive directors will recommend.[6]

The agreement to include the study of the reform of the rules and practices of the fund came only
after an eleventh-hour rift had threatened the approval of the outline establishing the SDR facility.
The controversy centered on the question of whether
or not agreement on the contingency reform plan were
linked with a reform of certain of the fund's rules
and practices. As usual, the EEC countries were
lined up on one side of the question (they insisted
that both reforms were in fact connected), and the
five "liberals" were lined up on the other side of
the issue. The latter felt that fund reform was no
precondition for international monetary reform.
Rather, such proposals would, after appropriate
study, be judged on their own merits and be accepted,
rejected, or altered on this basis.

When the six Common Market countries were
united, however, there was very little the United
States could do to impose its will. The fund reform
issue was no exception. When the executive directors
finalized the SDR agreement in early April, 1968,
included in the proposal was a series of suggested
modifications in the existing rules and practices of
the fund. The more important reforms recommended
included making the gold tranche fully automatic
and not subject to any prior challenge by the fund.
Another provision called for a small interest rate
to be paid on the so-called supergold-tranche position, which represents a member's net-creditor position. It is derived from extensive drawings of its
currency by other members.

More important are the changes proposed in
voting majorities. An 85 percent weighted majority
will apply to decisions on (1) general quota increases, (2) the terms and conditions associated with
such increases, (3) uniform proportionate changes
in par values, and (4) waiver of maintenance of value
of the fund's assets in the case of a uniform change
in par values. The proposal on general quota increases was desired by the French and the Belgians
to insure that the 85 percent majority for activating
and allocating SDR's could not be circumvented in
part by simply raising traditional fund quotas.

The effect of the increases in majorities for
uniform proportionate changes in par values and the

waiver of the gold-value maintenance of the fund's
assets is to fix more firmly the official price of
gold by giving the veto over a decision to increase
that price to the EEC as well as the United States.
All of the voting changes, admitted the House Banking and Currency Committee in its report on enabling
legislation clearly "reflect a strengthening of the
position of the countries of the European Economic
Community within the fund."

In fact, most of the fund reform proposals had
been drafted by the EEC's Monetary Committee and
approved by a meeting of its finance ministers in
Paris on December 14-15, 1967.

The interpretation of the nature and significance
of the agreement on SDR's varied from country to country. Both France and the United States claimed vic-
tory for their policies. After the decisive London
meeting, Fowler rejoiced over what had "indeed been
one of the great days in the history of financial cooperation." The United States further contended that
all of its primary objectives had been achieved. The
new SDR's would in fact be a "first-line reserve asset" and a fallback international currency that would
have all the characteristics of a full-scale reserve.
It was later emphasized that, up to 70 percent of its
usage, there was no real question but that the new
SDR's were a new form of international money. Whereas the French won the battle of semantics, the United
States felt that it had won the battle of substance.

The French were equally insistent that the SDR
agreement was tantamount to "a success for the French
thesis." This, because "the question of creating new
international money was discarded." At Rio, Debre asserted that his country, ever vigilant against "theories and fancies," had consented only "to a possible
mechanism for new credits, accompanied by a reform of
the IMF, and nothing more." SDR's, it was argued, in
no way constituted a "revolutionary step." They "do
not and cannot establish a new currency designed to
replace gold. If such were the purport of the agreement, it is quite clear that France would not sign
it." SDR's were therefore looked upon as providing
only for the "possible extending of credit facilities."

The Germans, still faithful to their French allies, argued at Rio that the new mechanism for the
expansion of liquidity was based on the principles of
credit and repayability. "As in the national field,

money is created by credit. So these new drawing
rights shall be controlled by volume and speed in
their creation."

On the other hand, the ever-pragmatic Italians
preferred to simply note that the outline represented
"a compromise between divergent and, at times, completely contrasting attitudes, whose supporters have
somehow managed to find common ground for agreement
in the fact of practical realities."

In the absence of the linguistic pragmatism and
semantic legerdemain existent in the outline approved
at London and again in Rio, it is not altogether
impossible that the Group of Ten might today still be
negotiating a monetary reform agreement. The equiv-
ocal and imprecise terminology used to describe SDR's
allowed all of the participants to interpret the
agreement in terms of their own policies and preju-
dices. Each delegation could return home and reasonably report that the new arrangement conformed to its
own national specifications. As long as the reform
plan were accepted and put into operation, it did not
really matter whether the ministers and governors
thought of the allocation of SDR's as extension of
credit, as creation and distribution of money, or as
any other financial hocus-pocus. "The system can work
to the satisfaction of anyone concerned even if the
disagreement on the economic character and economic
function of the SDR's continues."[7] Although
economists by profession, the architects of the international monetary reform plan displayed not insignificant political savvy.

The conflict between the French embrace of credit
extension and the U.S. insistence on full-fledged reserve units was resolved "by extraordinarily efficient
mediators applying the recipe of avoiding all the
words which the nations had written on their banners
and for which they were valiantly battling." The outline is, as a result, able to describe SDR's without
use of such seemingly basic and essential terms as
credit, reserve asset, credit facility, reserve units,
borrowed reserves, loans, and repayments. "Words not
burdened with a history of controversy, not associated with recognizable ideologies, and not widely used
in monetary theories, words, therefore, with still
neutral and not always fixed connotations were put in
place of the old, battle-scarred, and now banished
words."[8]

Perhaps the best description of the true nature of SDR's was made by Emminger, one of its founding fathers. He equated SDR's with a zebra "so that one can say they are a black animal with white stripes and another can say they are a white animal with black stripes."

COMPLETION OF THE RIO
AGREEMENT, MARCH, 1968

If the London ministerial meetings of the Group of Ten were the climax of the international monetary reform talks, then the ministerial meeting held on March 29-30, 1968, in Stockholm, was the anticlimax.

When the IMF's board of governors had approved the outline at Rio, it had hoped that the executive directors, acting alone, would be able to complete the formal, legal text of the necessary amendments to the fund's Articles of Agreement and By-laws. These amendments would formally establish the special drawing account and those modifications in the rules and practices of the fund which the executive directors would recommend. March 31, 1968, had been set by the governors as the deadline for the completion of this task. Accordingly, the executive directors had begun the final drafting immediately after the annual meeting in Rio ended.

However, a number of technical issues in the outline plan could not be resolved, principally the question of "opting out," i.e., a member country's removing itself from the obligation to participate in the SDR agreement once it was approved.

The Stockholm meeting rapidly assumed overtones of a suspenseful melodrama. No one really knew for sure if the French would in fact give their final approval at this late date to the SDR plan. And no one really knew the strength of France's diplomatic position vis-à-vis Germany, Italy, and the Benelux countries. If France rejected the plan, there was the distinct possibility that, in deference to EEC unity, these countries would effect a last-minute postponement of final agreement.

There were six issues before the ministers and governors at Stockholm on the SDR plan itself and

three issues connected with the reform of the fund.
Opting out was the major question left open in the
outline agreement and the only major substantive decision made at Stockholm to alter what had been approved
at Rio. The French were given their way on the opt-
ing-out procedure. An IMF member country agreeing to
participate in the reform plan which might be in opposition to the later decision to activate SDR's was
empowered to disassociate itself (at any time) from
the distribution of the new asset and of all obligations to accept SDR's in exchange for convertible
currencies. Having done so, a country still could
later change its mind and "opt in." The accomoda-
tion made on this issue, Under Secretary of the
Treasury Frederick Deming told a Congressional committee, "was frankly for the purpose of helping France
to participate in the plan."

Despite the "violent and obstructionist tactics"
of Debre, who wanted to discuss sweeping changes in
the international monetary system and a realistic
price for gold, final agreement was reached on the SDR
plan. The final agreement was, however, subscribed
to by only nine countries. France had in the end
refused to officially endorse the reform plan. Technically, it reserved its position at least until after
reading the final text of the proposed SDR amendment.
Said the final communiqué:

> One delegation did not associate it-
> self with [the substance of the com-
> muniqué] in view of the differences
> which it has found between the out-
> line adopted at the meetings in Lon-
> don and Rio de Janeiro and the draft
> text now submitted by the fund, and
> because the problems which it con-
> siders fundamental have not been
> examined.
>
> Consequently, this delegation fully
> reserves its position and will wait
> until it is in possession of the
> final texts before reporting to its
> government.[9]

The communiqué also noted that the ministers and
governors had approved the proposed changes in some
of the fund's rules and practices. Finally, the ministers and governors had given their countries'

executive directors in the IMF the "necessary authority" to work with the other executive directors
to complete the final draft of the proposed amendments on SDR's and fund reform.

The French had not firmly closed the door on
eventual participation in the monetary reform plan.
But this did not alter the fact that at the last minute there was no unanimity in the Group of Ten or in
the EEC. The finance ministers of the latter group
had held a caucus dinner on the eve of the Stockholm
meeting to consider their differences and once again
attempt to adopt a common position within the Group
of Ten. The attempt at unity was a failure.

The economic significance of Stockholm--the
clearing of the last real obstacle to agreement on
the SDR plan--was overshadowed by the political spectacle of France's flaunting the will of the majority
and determinedly moving into a temporary self-imposed
isolation from both its Atlantic, and, more impor-
tantly, its fellow Common Market countries. In the
last analysis, unity among the six could not withstand the objections of one country which threatened
to undo four-and-one-half years of work. It was too
late for French second thoughts to delay agreement
on the contingency reform plan desired by the rest
of the Group of Ten.

France apparently had crossed a threshold which
required its five partners to place national interests before community interests. Although the EEC
had been endeavoring for well over a year to achieve
a common position in the Group of Ten, the political
pride and leverage associated with such unity could
not in the end survive France's defiant determination
to go it alone. Unhappily for the six, they had
graphically proved the limitations of their ability
to act in unison.

Just two weeks behind schedule, the executive
directors (on April 16) completed the final details
of the full text of the monetary reform and fund reform agreements. They then submitted it to the board
of governors for approval by May 31. The "Report by
the Executive Directors to the Board of Governors
Proposing Amendment of the Articles of Agreement"
easily received the required approval by a simple
majority of the weighted votes cast by the governors
(France and fifteen members of the franc zone ab-
stained).

RATIFICATION AND IMPLEMENTATION
OF THE SPECIAL DRAWING RIGHTS PLAN

With the completion of both the drafting process
and the internal IMF clearance procedure, the monetary
reform plan was submitted to the governments of the
fund's members for ratification. To enter into effect, the proposed amendment to that organization's
Articles of Agreement had to be ratified by 65 countries having 80 percent of the total voting power.
In addition, members with at least 75 percent of the
vote had to deposit with the fund a written instrument stipulating acceptance, in accordance with
national law, of all the obligations of a participant
in the new special drawing account, i.e., acceptance
and use of SDR's. By June, 1968, the first notices
of ratification and instruments of acceptance were
received by the fund. Quick Congressional action
permitted the United States to be among the first
countries to give approval.

Ironically, it was the ratification of Belgium,
the Group of Ten country most sympathetic with de
Gaulle's liquidity policies, which provided the requisite margin to enable the special drawing account
and the various reforms of IMF procedures to take
effect on July 28, 1969. Ratification of the SDR
amendment did not itself commit IMF members to participate in the still inactive special drawing account. Only a notice of participation could do this.
Furthermore, no country could actually become a participant until countries representing 75 percent of
the total voting power had deposited written instruments of participation. This provision assured that
a viable number of countries would be committed to
the operation of the SDR plan before it could be implemented. On August 7, the necessary number of
instruments had been received, and by the time of the
annual meeting, in late September, some 74 fund members (of a total 111) had accepted the obligations
of participation.

The monetary reform plan was now mechanically
complete with one exception: A decision that allocation of a specific amount of SDR's was necessary.
This procedure is initiated nominally when the fund's
managing director, having become convinced that a
worldwide liquidity shortage exists, conducts "such

consultations as will enable him to ascertain that
there is broad support among the participants for the
allocation of special drawing rights at the proposed
rate and for the proposed period." Translated into
power politics, however, this statement means that
when the Group of Ten gives an okay to the Fund on
when and how to proceed, the managing director sub-
mits the allocation proposal for a vote. Assuming
an affirmative vote by countries having 85 percent
of the weighted voting power among the participants
in the plan (in deference to the EEC's 16.5 percent),
final approval for implementation of the reform plan
is obtained.

From 1963 through 1969, one constant of the reform exercise was the retention of ultimate power in
the international monetary decisionmaking process
squarely within the Group of Ten. Nation-states are
still loathe to relinquish to international organizations any real power in areas where important national-
sovereignty considerations are involved. And the control of international liquidity is an issue directly
touching on a major national interest. History repeated itself in the summer of 1969, as the Group of
Ten hastened to reach a consensus so that a prepack-
aged arrangement could be presented for formal approval during the IMF's annual meeting, traditionally
held in the fall. In 1967, it was the outline of a
contingency plan that was being debated. Two years
later, it was the real thing--physical distribution
of the new reserve asset.

The agreement which the Group of Ten reached in
the summer of 1967 and which was formally ratified by
the fund's entire membership two years later was a
contingency plan. The timing and magnitude of the
initial SDR allocation were left unresolved. For the
United States and most of the non-EEC countries, distribution of SDR's could come neither too soon nor in
too great a quantity. And thus, in 1969, the United
States again repeated its familiar task of taking the
argument of the impending need for deliberate-reserve
creation to the always-cautious Europeans. The fact
that the Group of Ten and not the IMF would make the
crucial decisions in the monetary reform exercise was
also unchanged. It was the deputies who met during
the first half of 1969 to establish some generally
acceptable guidelines for the desired amount of liquidity increases in the 1970's.

The last stage of negotiations was conducted, however, in an environment very dissimilar to the period which preceded the Rio meeting. In the first place, de Gaulle had ingloriously stepped down as France's President, gold was now flowing out of the French Treasury, and France as a whole was still staggering from the dislocations induced by the civil unrest and strikes of the previous spring. In short, sudden and severe economic weakness had forced France to step down from the triumverate of supermonetary decisionmakers. A smaller and more compatible diumverate remained. Germany had the strongest currency in Europe--if not the world--in early 1969, but it shared the universal shock at the intensity of the lightning turnabout in France's economy ("there but for the grace of God").

In the second place, the EEC countries, except Germany, continued to lose dollar balances (primarily to the high-yielding Eurodollar market) at the same time that aggregate official gold holdings in the Group of Ten were all but declared static. When a private gold rush necessitated closing the gold pool in March, 1968, the official agreement was interpreted as directing the major economic countries to refuse to buy newly mined gold (in order to channel it into the newly segregated private gold market).

The ten were also dismayed at the intensity of speculative capital flows, inspired by anticipations of exchange-rate changes, which at this time were playing havoc with international monetary stability. All of these developments contributed to a European acceptance of an early and major allocation of SDR's which would have been unheard of had there not been a radical change in the 1965-67 situation. The deputies were consequently able to settle the final question of the magnitude of SDR distribution with relative simplicity and quickness.

The deputies considered a number of methods in their attempt to reach agreement on some objective measurement of the proper growth of liquidity. Because the level of aggregate free world liquidity was stagnant during the 1967-68 period, it was pretty well necessary to base estimates of desired-liquidity growth on projections of increased trade. The IMF later reported that the various estimations of annual liquidity needs for the next three to five years fell within a range of approximately $3.5 to $6 billion a

year. Most estimates (including the United States'
and the fund's) fell between $4 and $5 billion annually. It further estimated that from $1 to $1.5
billion annually would be contributed to these totals
by traditional sources of reserves.

The resulting bargaining saw the EEC opt for an
initial annual allocation of $2 billion, twice the
amount of their 1966-67 preference and equal to the
more liberal U.S. preference at that time. The new
Under Secretary of the Treasury for Monetary Affairs,
Paul A. Volcker, countered with a $4 to $5 billion
proposal. On the first day of the deputies' session
held in late July, the numerical differences between
the two positions narrowed. Each side by now had
agreed that a "front-load" principle should be adopted
to assure a disproportionately large initial SDR allocation. Secondly, it was agreed that since the
total amount of SDR's which were to be created was a
matter of central concern, the length of the distribution period should be compromised rather than the
annual allocation figure. Allocations were therefore
projected for only three years instead of five. As
the meeting ended, the U.S. position was lowered to
$4 billion per year, while the EEC raised its posi-
tion to $2.5 billion. Japan supported a $3 to $4
billion figure.

On the second day of the meeting, the mutually
agreeable formula was finally reached. It retained
both the three-year and the "front-load" principles.
A total $3.5 billion would be allocated for 1970,
and $3 billion in each of the two succeeding years.
After this relatively brief period, the SDR operation
would be reassessed. However, no public announcement
was made of the decision. The ten diplomatically
left it to the fund's Managing Director Schweitzer
to make the formal proposal, on September 23, that
the first of three annual allocations of SDR's be
made on January 1, 1970. It might also be noted here
that France, the lone Group of Ten country to withhold approval of the agreement, quietly participated
in the aforementioned deputies' meetings. Its presence was rationalized in part by virtue of having
placed a few minor matters, unrelated to international
monetary reform, on the deputies' agenda. (The French
Parliament subsequently approved that country's participation in the plan). The Group of Ten having already reached agreement, the official vote of sanc-
tion by the IMF's board of governors was an event

whose outcome was never in doubt. On October 3, the
"necessary majority" was obtained (73 yeas and South
Africa abstaining). The international monetary reform plan was now ready for implementation.

The initial allocation of SDR's was made in the
internal books of the IMF, as scheduled, on the first
day of 1970. The equivalent of $3.41 billion was al-
located to 104 participants. One of the would-be
participants, Nationalist China, which has seldom
utilized its relatively large quota, opted out of
that year's allocation. It therefore received neither
its $90 million allocation nor any of the obligations
of the plan. Ten of the IMF's current total of 115
members still had not deposited their instruments of
participation and consequently were not eligible to
receive SDR's. All were small states, and at least
eight could be categorized as having plentiful gold
and dollar reserves. Such countries as Kuwait, Saudi
Arabia, Libya, Lebanon, Singapore, and Portugal were
more likely to be recipients than users of SDR's in
1970. Apparently they preferred not to be faced with
the probable obligation to exchange some of their
existing reserves for SDR's. France and South Africa
were participants.

Because SDR allocations were proportionate (17
percent). to regular IMF quotas--and thus ultimately
to economic significance--on the last day of 1970,.
the Group of Ten accounted for a disproportionately
large amount (65 percent) of total SDR's received.
Individual allocations ranged from the equivalent of
$867 million to the United States, $410 million to
the United Kingdom, $165 million to France, $122
million to Japan, $59 million to Brazil, all the way
down to $500,000 to the small African states of
Botswana and Lesotho.

The preparations for the first structural reform
of the post-World War II international monetary system are now over. Nevertheless, formal consideration
of further reforms, such as increased exchange-rate
flexibility and crawling pegs, is almost sure to follow in the 1970's. Indeed, the IMF is already examining the technical aspects of these issues. And the
finance ministers and central bank governors of the
Group of Ten countries have bade their deputies continue their regular meetings "for the purpose of re-
viewing developments, and possible improvements, in
the functioning of the international monetary system."

NOTES

1. Agence Internationale D'Information pour la Presse, Europe, Daily Bulletin No. 2664, April 18, 1967, p. 1 (underscoring supplied).

2. Ibid.

3. The American Banker, July 25, 1967.

4. "Communiqué of the Ministerial Meeting of the Group of Ten on August 26, 1967, London," U.S. Treasury Department, Press Release dated August 28, 1967, pp. 1-2.

5. Ibid.

6. International Monetary Fund, "Summary Proceedings," Twenty-Second Annual Meeting, 1967 (Washington, D.C.: The Fund, 1968), pp. 271-72.

7. Fritz Machlup, Remaking the International Monetary System (Baltimore: Johns Hopkins Press, 1968), pp. 94-95.

8. Ibid., p. 9.

9. International Monetary Fund, International Financial News Survey, XX, 13 (April 5, 1968), p. 1.

6

THE POLITICAL
MEANING OF THE
MONETARY
REFORM PLAN

Although far from operating according to what
was originally envisioned by its drafters in 1944
and much maligned as being neither equitable nor
technically sound, the gold-exchange standard has
left the free world a lasting legacy of prosperity.
The fortuitous combination of an open-ended U.S.
balance-of-payments deficit and an equally open-ended
worldwide demand for dollars was the catalytic agent
for a postwar pattern of economic growth in the North
Atlantic region which is probably without precedent.
Emminger appropriately asked in a 1966 speech whether
the monetary system, despite being talked to pieces,
had not in fact fostered an "almost unbroken rise,
unique in economic history," of the world economy
for the past fifteen years. "Whatever the weaknesses
of this international monetary order may be, in comparison to earlier monetary systems--the old gold
currency before 1914 not excluded--this system has
still proved itself the best."

A SUMMING UP

The contemporary international monetary system
is therefore not without great successes. But something has gone wrong with it. Crisis has followed
crisis, and people who did not even know there was
such a thing as an international monetary system were
suddenly made aware of the U.S. gold drain, currency
speculations, and other esoteric items previously
confined to technical journals and the financial pages
of The New York Times.

The mainstay of postwar international finance
has been the U.S. dollar. Representing the largest
national economy in the world and freely convertible
into gold by central banks at $35 an ounce, the dol-
lar was considered for a time to be "as good as gold."
Then, like threads in a knitted sweater, the system
began to unravel. A chain of incompatible events had
been set in motion. U.S. balance-of-payments deficits
of the 1950's were compatible with U.S. political-
economic hegemony, and everything went along fine
while it lasted. But once this hegemony diminished,
the combination of European revitalization and persistent balance-of-payments surpluses became incompatible
with the persistent U.S. deficit. In turn, resulting
U.S. losses of gold were incompatible with a continuation of the dollar's reserve and commercial supremacy. Elimination of the U.S.-payments deficit became
mandatory for global monetary stability. However,
limited availabilities of newly mined gold and the
anticipation of the dollar drain's demise were incompatible with the anticipated need for increased
liquidity in a growing world economy. The resulting
need to create a new reserve unit, directly touching
as it did on national sovereignty and national interests, was incompatible with a technician's search
for the economically optimal in a political vacuum.
A reform was necessary, however, inasmuch as a monetary status quo was incompatible with the European
determination to achieve parity with the once-omni-
potent United States in the management and control of
international liquidity.

In short, the monetary system is a mirror of the
international balance of political power. Because the
latter partially reflects economic strength, reserve
balances become a form of political power. And it has
been continental Western Europe that, since the
1950's, has had the greatest quantitative increase
in its monetary reserves.

The gold-exchange standard constructed at Bretton
Woods was born into a very simplistic free world,
balance-of-power structure. At the same time, however, it contained a very delicate structural complexity. The monetary system was highly dependent
on an adequate supply of foreign-held reserve-currency
balances, while simultaneously being highly nervous
at the prospect of having excessive balances of reserve currency outstanding. But an optimal amount of

liquidity producing a perfect balancing of supply and
confidence was as much a long shot as a permanent
political domination of Europe by the United States.
Once Triffin began eloquently enunciating the problem
in 1959, monetary complacency gradually yielded to
uneasiness and finally to contingency planning.

Significantly, the early warnings preceded by
only a few months the crucial transition of the
world's major reserve-currency country from the
status of international creditor to a net, short-term
international debtor. The technical underpinnings of
the gold-exchange standard were forever changed.
What was once a sizable, albeit technically and politically inconsequential U.S. balance-of-payments
deficit now forced this country's creditors to re-
assess the make-up of their total monetary reserves.
Although a handful of countries accounted for the
bulk of the dollar accumulations, cries of a worldwide liquidity surplus were quite prevalent in Atlantic monetary literature. For political and economic
reasons, continued increases in dollar holdings became a source of discomfort for six central banks.

The U.S. Government tried a myriad of policy de-
vices to make good on its commitment to eliminate its
seemingly interminable external deficit. However,
neither it nor its European creditors appreciated or
anticipated the intractability of a politically induced deficit in a capital-exporting country. With
certain foreign and domestic policy commitments given
priority over balance-of-payments equilibrium, the
dollar outflow and the gold drain, like "Ol' Man
River," just kept rolling along.

As the ratio of this country's gold stock to
external-liquid liabilities to foreigners deterio-
rated, political cooperation became mandatory to maintain the stability of the monetary system. A number
of ad-hoc arrangements were devised in an effort to
provide a semblance of business as usual. Everyone
continued to believe that in just a few more months
the long-anticipated end of the U.S. deficit would
come about. However, there could be few sighs of
genuine relief at this prospect. Together with the
unanimously agreed fact that new stocks of monetary
gold were unlikely to adequately meet the demand for
future liquidity increments, the prospect of the dollar drain's end brought the gold-exchange standard to
a fork in the roads. Choosing to ignore the path to

a slow death by strangulation, the monetary officials
of the ten leading Western economic powers took the
path to reform.

In view of European attitudes and ambitions,
creation of a new form of deliberately created liquidity to supplement the traditional forms of monetary
reserves was obviously necessary. Although an intel-
lectually challenging task, the need by some of the
world's best economic brains to labor more than four
years to agree on the form of this new asset can only
be explained by viewing the question of international
liquidity creation as one which transcends economic
theory.

Since liquidity is used for the immediate, technical purpose of financing balance-of-payments deficits and postponing the need for restrictive and
deflationary governmental economic policies which
tend to retard economic growth, it is possible to
use nothing but economic terms and concepts to describe the actual utilization of international liquidity. However, such a treatment cannot provide a
full comprehension of the subject. No economist has
been bold enough to declare that he knows definitely
the exact quantity of liquidity to assure balanced
growth in the prevailing volume of world trade. Leading scholars in this field readily admitted that one's
belief as to needs was a political opinion reflective
of differing values. Abstract economic theory can no
more explain the guts of international monetary reform than can purely military terms explain the mal-
aise of NATO.

The monetary reform talks are best understood
only when considered not as an isolated series of
financial discussions but as an offspring of Atlantic
community political dynamics. They are actually a
financial manifestation of the most basic contemporary phenomenon within that so-called community: the
drive by the rejuvenated countries of Western Europe
to upset the postwar status quo which reflects the
one-time political, military, and economic hegemony
of the United States in the Atlantic Alliance.

The changing environment of the liquidity talks
was admirably summarized by the man probably most
disenchanted with that status quo, Charles de Gaulle:

As the Western European States, destroyed and ruined by the wars,

recover their substance, their
relative situation following their
debilitation appears inadequate,
even abusive and dangerous. More-
over, nothing in this statement
implies that they, particularly
France, are in any way unfriendly
toward other countries, especially
toward America. For the fact that
these States wish, more each day,
to act independently in every
field of international relations
is due merely to the nature of
things.[1]

In short, de Gaulle's liquidity policies were predicated on the belief that the circumstances which
justified the prominence of the dollar were no longer
appropriate guidelines for action: "Times have
changed and so has the system."

The inevitable turning point in the gold-exchange
standard was greatly hastened by two interrelated
factors: the persistent U.S. balance-of-payments deficit and the equally persistent surpluses of many of
the Western European countries. For a variety of economic, political, and psychological reasons, the exact
blend of which varied from country to country, the
Europeans began to exchange a growing percentage of
the new dollar balances accumulated by their central
banks for U.S. gold. If the United States had possessed an infinite supply of gold, if the Europeans
had not maintained such large surpluses, or if the
Europeans had more patience with the United States,
the international monetary crisis would not have come
in the 1960's. None of these contingencies, of
course, were ever realized.

The need for the United States to eliminate its
external deficit is commonly described in the most
somber of technical terms. Almost never are the
liquidity-producing, private capital-producing, military protection-producing effects of the deficit given
the benefit of the doubt or spoken of in positive
terms. Equally rare is a forthright public admission,
domestically or in Europe, that the uniquely political
sources of this payments deficit are somewhat imper-
vious to the basic tenets of the adjustment process,
such as deflationary monetary and fiscal policies.
Instead of publicly arguing that U.S. investment in

Europe had to be checked or that U.S. overseas military commitments were excessive, the continental critics--especially outside of France--constructed their arguments in terms of exported inflation, the need for monetary discipline, and so forth. The immediate target of their wrath was the deficit, but the source of that wrath was the policies contributing to it and the power emanating from it.

It must again be emphasized that there are two sides to the balance-of-payments equation. Under existing guidelines, chronic-surplus countries are themselves in disequilibrium. As such, they are in theory dutybound to restore equilibrium to their balance of payments. However, accumulation of reserve assets does not have nearly the discipline-inducing effect as asset losses. Feeling no responsibility to adopt expansionary policies, the European surplus countries reap substantial political mileage by placing the responsibility for international monetary stability squarely into this country's lap. The potential, domestic-economic rewards for lowered import duties or a revalued currency is a growth in real income or an improvement in the terms of trade which would result from imports being made available more cheaply. The Europeans, for their part, were more concerned with the political penalties of surplus termination: forfeiture of the considerable leverage associated with large reserve holdings and the chance to "twit the Americans."

It is an overstatement of the case to imply that unrequited financing ad nauseam of the Anglo-Saxons' deficits by the EEC countries is attractive on either technical or altruistic terms. It is not. Nevertheless, a full comprehension of the complex and interconnected problems of the international monetary system defies a simple arithmetic comparison of the deteriorating ratio of U.S. gold to foreign short-term liabilities. The critical question is not the size of the liabilities but the attitudes of dollar holders.

The Chairman of the 1965 Study Group on the Creation of Reserve Assets, Rinaldo Ossola, placed the monetary problem in the following political perspective:

> It must be stated that the liquidity
> needs of the international economy is

not a concept that belongs to the economic categories. This need cannot be
assessed unless the desire of national
monetary authorities to preserve a margin of autonomy in conducting their
economic policy is taken into account.
Those mainly interested in the solution of this problem are obviously the
industrial countries which, being the
major holders of real resources, have
to weigh whether, and within what limits,
they are prepared to grant one another
reciprocally an automatic and unconditional right to draw on their resources.
The problem is therefore essentially of
a political nature. The experts can
indicate the alternative solutions,
their effects on the functioning of the
international monetary system, and their
significance in terms of shifts of real
resources, a development underlying the
monetary process. Obviously, however,
they cannot make or propose any choice.[2]

As did most of the other senior participants in
the talks, former French Finance Minister Debre agreed
with Ossola's implication that international monetary
reform was intrinsically a political process. "Any
important problem is political, and cannot be otherwise," he told an interviewer. The monetary system
was born out of and then functioned from a series of
circumstances that were political as much as economic.
Debre also said that "The criticism of the gold-exchange standard, made so often in the past few years,
goes beyond the technical field into the political
field."[3]

Excess liquidity has been confined to the continent of Western Europe. Literally dozens of poorer
countries, less concerned with achieving a power
parity via-à-vis the United States and less able to
afford to yield the purchasing power of interest-
bearing dollars for relatively sterile gold, would
have welcomed additional dollar balances even in 1970.

The challenge to the dollar becomes considerably
more clear when European attitudes, which have been
elaborated on in preceeding chapters, are contrasted
with what might be termed the brief for the majority.
The latter was delivered in its best form during the

1965 IMF annual meeting by the Chairman of Denmark's
central bank, Erik Hoffmeyer. He stated that his
country's low preference for gold was based on neither lack of insight in international payments problems nor lack of means to finance the holding of
gold. "The rationale for continuing an exchange reserve policy is that international cooperation will
prove that in the long run it is of no great importance whether we hold our reserves in gold or in
foreign exchange." It was his view that the future
stability of the present system would be dependent
upon the willingness of the "gold countries" to reduce their preference for gold.[4]

Continued acceptance of dollars as a source of
new liquidity could be anticipated only under the
dubious assumption that European governments were
prepared to relinquish the considerable degree of
national sovereignty implicit in any abandonment to
the U.S. political and commercial sectors of control
over the management and use of their monetary reserves. It is therefore difficult to imagine European
willingness to blindly underwrite future U.S. balance-
of-payments deficits, irrespective of their amounts
and of the sometimes political cause of their emergence and continuance. Given the absence of a political consensus, the only practical way to maintain
a European-approved deficit would be for the United
States to confer upon its European creditors a veto
right on its own internal and external policies inso-
far as the latter might determine the increase of
U.S.-dollar liabilities to European central banks.

To the extent that Hans Morgenthau is correct
in his contention that the essence of international
politics is a struggle for power, it can be asserted
that the essence of the monetary reform exercise was
international politics. At the very heart of the
European-U.S. dialogue on liquidity was the drive for
international monetary power: the power to prolong
policies that contribute to payments deficits and the
power to control the ability of other countries to
sustain payments deficits and the policies inducing
them. Once political and economic vitality was restored to the continent which gave birth to power
politics, it was all but axiomatic that it would take
steps to recover the national sovereignty and power
relinquished to the United States in the immediate
postwar period.

The nation or nations that control the form and
issuance of international reserves possesses a significant amount of indirect political and direct economic power. Once upon a time, there were no objections
to the United States alone possessing this power and
reaping its rewards. The rest of the world was weak
and needed dollars. But then another area of the
world became very strong. By accumulating large dollar balances, in effect U.S. IOU's, these countries
assumed a degree of economic power very nearly as
large as that of the principal issuer of new international liquidity. The absence of a true political
community between the United States and Western
Europe produced a power struggle over the question of
liquidity control. Shared control then became the
principal ingredient of changing the structure of the
gold-exchange standard. This is a simple concept,
but the absence of an American-European consensus on
economic strategy and objectives made necessary four-
and-one-half years of talk to construct the mechanics
of shared control.

Despite its technical veneer, liquidity is clearly political when the unquestioned reserve role of the
dollar both subsidizes this country's pursuit of political-economic policies unacceptable to its European
creditors and enables the United States to almost unilaterally determine the annual expansions of international liquidity. The access to liquidity is, in
short, a source of autonomy to pursue national policy
priorities, domestic and foreign, and the means to be
a net borrower of other countries' economic resources.
When it is further considered that the resulting attempt to negotiate a maximization of value ends was
made in the midst of conflicting frames of reference,
the liquidity question can reasonably be placed
squarely under the rubric of politics.

The idea of permitting a further infringement by
the United States on their sovereignty was totally re-
pugnant to the Europeans. They simply refused to ac-
quiesce in the preservation of an old order, an order
which they regarded as bestowing an intolerable power
and prestige on the United States. In his widely
read book, Henry A. Kissinger wrote that the cause of
the Atlantic problem was the result of three factors:
the need for centralized control, the desire of each
major ally to have substantial influences on common
decisions, and the wish of the major allies to share
in the prestige and political power which control

confers or is thought to confer. He further wrote
that the dilemma arose because there was no scheme
which could reconcile these objectives perfectly as
long as the Atlantic Alliance remained composed of
sovereign states. The only political solution that
could resolve the inevitable clash of interests would
be establishment of a supranational authority to replace national decisionmakers.[5]

Kissinger was not writing about monetary reform.
He was actually writing about NATO's "nuclear dilemma." Yet, the terminology, causes, and cure of the
nuclear problem are indistinguishable from the international liquidity problem. The reason is simple:
They are both manifestations of the changing balances
of power in the Atlantic community and the European
determination to reorient their position vis-à-vis
the United States consistent with this shift.

The only major difference between the liquidity
and the nuclear problems is that the Europeans can do
nothing to wrest the nuclear monopoly from the United
States other than undertaking the costly effort of
building their own national or regional nuclear deter-
rent. With respect to the liquidity problem, the
Europeans have very real power: potential claims on
the U.S.-gold supply. In theory at least, the chief
foreign creditors of the United States have the power
to foment a widespread collapse of confidence in the
dollar which could temporarily or permanently disrupt
international trade and payments. Although the EEC
countries had exploited with ruthless efficiency the
gold-exchange standard's inherent weaknesses, the
absence of any conceivable gains by actually attempting to deplete the U.S.-gold supply has heretofore
precluded any mass European move in this direction.
Undoubtedly, this reflects the concept that nations
cooperate primarily because they have common purposes,
not because they have a legal obligation to do so.

The fact still remained, though, that the Europeans now had the power to precipitate an international monetary crisis that might deal a lethal blow
to the special role of the dollar, a role which the
U.S. Government wishes to preserve. The continued
operation of the system became dangerously dependent
on voluntary cooperation among central banks and
vulnerable to European tactics designed to apply
pressure on the United States to adhere to balance-
of-payments policies desired by its creditors. An

increase in the price of gold, the "other" reserve
component, might have bought a little extra time.
However, this possibility was unequivocally opposed
by all free world countries except France (and South
Africa).

The only feasible solution was creation of a new
form of international liquidity. In what might be
termed a classic example of economic power politics,
the Group of Ten simply took it upon themselves to
devise such a new asset. Their acceptance of the
responsibility to create a monetary reform plan reflected their feeling that assuring adequate reserves
was a problem peculiar to their large and sophisticated economies. Economic aid and development was
considered a totally separate subject, bearing little
or no relationship to their chosen task. The early
reform proposals--increased swap networks, mutual
currency holdings, and creation of a composite reserve unit--all were at first blush merely simple
extensions of the ad hoc efforts at Atlantic monetary
cooperation. The fundamental economic problem of
Asia, Africa, and Latin America was deemed to be a
shortage of development capital, a problem distinctly
different from the potential future shortage of the
means to finance temporary balance-of-payments deficits in countries heavily involved in a growing volume of trade.

The explanation as to why politics intruded into
and controlled the course of the monetary reform process leads to the question of how this influence manifested itself. Did not the course of the liquidity
talks in fact perfectly follow the script of the basic
pattern of Atlantic community politics: U.S. and
French policies at opposite ends of the spectrum, with
Germany's eclectic policy standing in between as a
reconciling middleman? Were there not also a series
of political influences which logically expressed the
desire of the EEC to maintain a unified position in
the Group of Ten talks, as well as the desire of the
less-developed countries and the IMF to have their
opinions on monetary reform carefully considered by
the Atlantic economic powers? The confirmation of
both assertions is readily apparent in an empirical
review of the liquidity talks' progress.

In the end, the plan agreed on was at the same
time limited enough to allow the French to proclaim
special drawing rights as mere extensions of international credit and liberal enough to allow the rest of

the world to be content in the knowledge that what in
fact had been created was extremely close to being a
full-fledged form of international money. It is highly doubtful, albeit conjectural, to assume that the
relatively innocuous reconstitution figure of 30
percent was much more than the price at which French
support could be bought. It is also doubtful, but
again conjectural, to assume that the French would
have received such a handsome tribute if it were not
for their extremely cagey and very effective use of
the principle of Common Market unity. As applied in
the EEC finance ministers' meetings, the resulting
leverage on France's partners, who were also the international balancers of financial power, greatly
strengthened that country's hand.

     The story of the monetary reform talks has many
lessons for the student of international politics as
well as the student of international economics. One
of the most important of these is the strengths and
weaknesses of the EEC. Whereas the academic phase
of the talks had been characterized by traditional
dynamics between sovereign nation-states, the political phase was characterized by relations between regular state actors (the United States to be precise)
and states which were an integral part of the EEC.
Once political decisions loomed on the horizon, the
latter no longer negotiated individually with out-
siders. Differences among the six were smoothed over
in private so that the community could speak with a
single voice in the Group of Ten talks. In unity
there would be strength.

     The economics of power had placed the decision-
making machinery for an issue of universal import
within the Group of Ten. In effect, it had become
the security council of the IMF. The U.N. Security
Council and the Group of Ten alike are dominated by
a very few "superpowers." The former is dominated
by the United States and the Soviet Union. In the
case of the latter, decisions on monetary reform were
ultimately in the hands of three major powers: the
United States, France, and Germany.

     What actually transpired was not so much a give-
and-take negotiation between three separate countries
but an exercise in uniting three concentric circles
with Germany as the connecting link. The Germans
shared the U.S. predilection for reaching agreement
on the creation of a relatively unrestricted reserve
asset but demanded that there be an unmistakably clear

provision of effective control by continental European countries. There were no serious obstacles to a quick, complete, economic meeting of the minds between the German and U.S. finance ministries other than the very important political factor of German desire for Common Market unity. The latter was, however, but a euphemism for the basic policy of all three of West Germany's chancellors: a firm continuation of Franco-German rapprochement and of the special relationship between the two countries as provided in the 1963 Franco-German Treaty of Cooperation.

The efforts of the EEC ministers to prepare a unified position on deliberate-reserve creation for presentation in the Group of Ten often presented the spectacle of a community in disarray. The fact that such basic decisions as the utilization of drawing rights with a reconstitution requirement rather than reserve units and also the provision of a blocking vote for the six were made within the EEC finance ministers' meetings attests to the power of a unified community determined to enforce a certain policy on the United States.

But once beyond the relatively easy agreement that no important decision could be made in the new plan over the opposition of a united EEC, little evidence existed of genuine harmony in these meetings. On two occasions, the dissident and overruled Italians and Dutch felt compelled to publicly assert that nothing in the meeting's final communiqué should be construed as meaning that any community position was irrevocably settled and not open to later revision. On more than one occasion, the Dutch and Italian financial ministers all but publicly decried the fact that the meetings of the EEC finance ministers had developed into a series of bilateral agreements between the Germans and the French in return for the latter's progressive abandonment of specious and untenable positions.

Significantly, most of the concessions made to the ultraconservative French were made within the councils of the Common Market and not in the Group of Ten. The French, very simply, used the bogey of unity to compel the Germans to present the Italians and the Dutch, when necessity required, with a fait accompli. The power of Franco-German compromise produced EEC unity, and the power of this unity in turn presented the rest of the Group of Ten a fait accompli.

The French could by no stretch of the imagination get everything they wanted. But the bond of their Common Market association produced for a country whose policy was out of the mainstream of thought a strength of bargaining power completely dispropor-tionate with either the strength of the French economy or the economic logic of the French position. As with so many other issues, France was the one country which most insisted on a unanimous EEC policy, not because of particular love for European unity, but because of a hope to impose its own policy views on its partners and then present them as community positions.

The international monetary reform talks also of-fered lessons to students of the foreign policies of the great powers. The origin of the reform exercise to a large extent lay in the Gaullist propensity of exploiting the inevitable and assailing what was wide-ly regarded in Western Europe as U.S. power so exces-sive that it was too great for anyone's good. As was pointed out by Debre, France was the first country to denounce the defects in the present system and to argue that it was inequitable and irrational as re-gards the creation of liquidity. But as is so often the case, Gaullist perceptiveness soon became over-whelmed by hyperbole and invective toward the Anglo-Saxons. The French had not constructed the monetary crisis. They simply exploited an inherently combus-tible situation. Once the General had fully entered the picture, however, France soon overplayed its position to the point where its allies were forced to disassociate themselves from that position.

Whereas the French were content to make life uncomfortable for the Anglo-Saxon reserve-currency countries, the rest of the Group of Ten identified with U.S. leadership in pressing for an early and effective solution to the problem which had been un-earthed. None could compare with France's clear and premeditated elevation of politics over economics.

The political basis of international monetary reform had been constructed on the political dynam-ics of Atlantic community politics. France and the United States were the antagonists, with the Germans,

having both a political and economic foot in each
camp, caught in the middle. U.S. power and prestige
are without equal in the Atlantic community. Nevertheless, it was German diplomacy which successfully
brought the French into line and assured acceptance
of the SDR plan so ardently supported by the United
States. During the monetary reform exercise, the
United States supplied the impetus and inspiration
for agreement. The Germans delivered the French.

Like its French adversary, U.S. monetary policy
was not without parallels to its other Atlantic
policies. In each case, an inability to accept the
fact that something fundamental had indeed changed
led to a misguided effort to alter the form of Atlantic cooperation--i.e., make U.S. hegemony less
conspicuous--without attacking the problem itself--
i.e., European desire for power and shared control.
As a consequence, Roosa's credit facilities and reciprocal currency holding plan were just as unsuccessful as the multilateral force in assuaging
European demands. It was not until after Treasury
Secretary Fowler felt assured that creation of a
jointly managed reserve asset would not jeopardize
the dollar's existing reserve role that a reform
plan could be negotiated with the Europeans.

Agreement was reached for the simple reason
that it was in the best interests of all the Atlantic
states to create a new source of international liquidity. The agreement probably would have been
neither so liberal nor reached so early had it not
been for the rigid determination of the U.S. Government to achieve a far-reaching reform plan, far in
advance of the contingency being planned for.

In retrospect, the denouement of the liquidity
talks was seemingly preordained. It was an almost
inevitable compromise between the Anglo-Saxon and
continental positions. Treasury Secretary Fowler
and his deputy, Under Secretary Deming, provided
critical injections of indefatigable determination
and measured use of U.S. power--particularly vis-à-
vis the Germans--which were instrumental in piercing
continental inertia and monetary conservatism. However, the United States did not talk the EEC countries into reforming the international monetary
system. They raised the issue in the first place.
What the United States did was to extend the continental fixation with ending this country's

balance-of-payments deficit so as to accept the need
for swiftly and adequately preplanning for the consequences of its end.

On the technical level, Emminger's competence
and dynamic leadership of the deputies throughout
the critical phase of their work were also in no
small way responsible for the success of the liquidity talks.

WHAT SPECIAL DRAWING RIGHTS
WILL AND WILL NOT DO

A final question which remains to be answered
deals with the correlation between the plan which
was agreed upon and the political phenomenon which
was its inspiration: the Europeans' determination
to achieve a parity with the United States in the
international monetary decisionmaking process which
would be reflective of their vastly increased political-economic power. An assessment of the significance
and impact of SDR's on the international monetary
system is a logical conclusion to this study.

The single most important characteristic of
the SDR plan is that it will provide a vehicle whereby the United States and Europe will be given shared
authority over the future creation and control of
international liquidity. Since SDR's will probably
have only a limited impact on moderating the restrictive discipline of the adjustment process in a system
of fixed-exchange rates, they will introduce only
nominal technical reforms into the monetary system.
To provide major technical reforms in the reaction
of domestic-economic policy to a payments deficit,
the new asset would have to provide a truly revolutionary alternative to the traditional forms of
monetary reserves. SDR's do not meet this basic
requirement. As a means of international payment,
they will bear striking similarities to old-fashioned
dollars and gold.

SDR's without doubt will bring many innovations
to international finance. Countries receiving them
will not have "earned" them in the traditional sense.
Secondly, the world will not be nearly so dependent
on a U.S. balance-of-payments deficit for its much
needed long-term growth in reserves. Thirdly, SDR's

will have their acceptance enforced by international
law; the obligation to accept gold and reserve currencies is purely voluntary. Finally, inasmuch as
the quantity of SDR's to be allocated will reflect
an international consensus, there should be little or
no loss of confidence in them as their amount outstanding grows.

Nevertheless, after SDR's are actually in the
hands of a given country, operational differences
will tend to disappear. Allocations of SDR's, like
accumulations of dollars, will have no direct correlation with national needs. Worldwide supplies of
the new asset will still be extremely scarce relative
to demand and need. Deficit countries will no more
be freed from the traditional balance-of-payments
discipline under the "reformed" system than under
the former one. SDR's will not make obsolete the
deflationary and restrictive policies which have the
effect of sacrificing domestic-economic growth to
international equilibrium considerations.

The Europeans will have a veto over the amount
of SDR allocations. Consequently, their relatively
rigid and conservative economic views may clash with
the majority of other countries which place primary
emphasis on economic growth, not economic discipline.
SDR's in theory may be created ad infinitum, but in
practice they will be issued in relatively restrictive amounts. The economics of balance-of-payments
discipline and adjustment will remain essentially
unchanged. Today's liquidity-starved nations, especially the less-developed ones, will find domestic
policies equally beholden to external-equilibrium
requirements as before. SDR's therefore are no technical panacea to the problem of reconciling domestic
and international economic policies. In this respect, they will be no different from traditional
reserves in providing only a brief interim cushion
for a deficit country until restrictive economic policies can take effect and restore a payments equilibrium.

Since the technical significance of SDR's is
secondary to their political significance, none of
the above should be construed as an argument that
no structural change was agreed to at Rio in the fall
of 1967. The fact is that where reform really occurred was in the political sector. The outstanding
effect of this round of monetary reform was a political transformation, not an economic revolution. The

nearly exclusive control by the United States of
international liquidity management shifted to the
status of a joint venture with Western Europe. The
structural change produced by the reform plan is to
be found in the manner in which liquidity is to be
administered and controlled, not in the nature of
the new asset. The supranational authority to replace national decisionmakers, which Kissinger
suggested as a remedy for NATO's nuclear sharing
problem, has been created. Activation of the SDR
facility means that the control, power, and prestige
associated with the issuance of new international
money no longer rests exclusively with the United
States.

The Europeans partially dethroned the dollar
but were faced with the problem of providing a re-
placement. The dollar has been the most widely used
and accepted national currency in the history of international finance, and the Europeans had neither
the desire nor the economic power to provide a national currency capable of serving as a full-fledged
partner for the dollar. To prevent an economic vacuum, their only recourse was to agree on the creation
of a reserve asset through an international organization in which they would have a decisionmaking
power equal to that of the United States.

The SDR facility will meet this requirement.
The SDR plan will be administered within the IMF.
It will also have a decisionmaking process whereby
both the activation of the facility and the decision
on the volume of drawing rights to be allocated will
be blocked if the six EEC countries vote as a unit.
Under the reformed system, these countries will join
the United States in the exclusive rank of super-
international-financial power. Presently based heavily on the balance-of-payments deficit of a single
country, the process of creating and controlling new
monetary reserves in the future will be internation-
alized under the auspices of an international organization.

The realities of national sovereignty had precluded monetary reform in a truly economic sense.
Only a quick and major abrogation of economic sovereignty could provide that still elusive "quantum
of international currency, which is neither determined in an unpredictable and irrelevant manner but
rather is governed by the actual current requirements
of world commerce, and is also capable of deliberate

expansion and contraction to offset deflationary and inflationary tendencies in effective world demand" called for in 1943 by John Maynard Keynes.[6] The worldwide supply of liquidity may or may not be in line with the need for it under the reform plan. The SDR facility will assure only a wider decisionmaking apparatus. It cannot assure wiser or more efficient decisions than existed when the unpredictable size of the U.S.-payments deficit was the prime determinant of new reserve creation. All it can provide is a political consensus.

Economic interdependence and interpenetration have produced a diminution of economic sovereignty in the Atlantic community. But until there is a spillover into the realm of political sovereignty, the Group of Ten and the IMF will be able to function as true supranational instruments only under the most restrictive of conditions. More than a quarter of a century later, the world and the Atlantic community still have not caught up with Keynes.

NOTES

1. "Excerpts From the Press Conference Held by General de Gaulle as President of the French Republic in Paris at the Elysée Palace on February 4, 1965," Press Release, French Embassy Press and Information Service, p. 1.

2. Rinaldo Ossola, "On the Creation of New Reserve Assets: The Report Of the Study Group of Ten," Banca Nazionale del Lavoro Quarterly Review, XVIII (September, 1965), 290-91.

3. Translated from Le Monde, January 8-9, 1969.

4. International Monetary Fund, "Summary Proceedings," Twentieth Annual Meeting, 1965 (Washington, D.C.: The Fund, 1966), p. 165.

5. Henry A. Kissinger, The Troubled Partnership (New York: Anchor Books, 1966).

6. John Maynard Keynes, "Proposals for an International Clearing Union," British Government White Paper (His Majesty's Stationery Office, Cmd 6437).

APPENDIX

APPENDIX

OUTLINE OF THE SPECIAL
DRAWING RIGHTS AGREEMENT*

Introduction

The facility described in this Outline is intended to meet the need, as and when it arises, for a supplement to existing reserve assets. It is to be established within the framework of the Fund and, therefore, by an Amendment of the Fund's Articles. Provisions relating to some of the topics in this Outline could be included in By-Laws adopted by the Board of Governors or Rules and Regulations adopted by the Executive Directors rather than in the Amendment.

I. Establishment of a Special Drawing Account in the Fund

A. An Amendment to the Articles will establish a Special Drawing Account through which all the operations relating to special drawing rights will be carried out. The purposes of the facility will be set forth in the introductory section of the Amendment.

B. The operations of and resources available under the Special Drawing Account will be separate from the operation of the present Fund which will be referred to as the General Account.

C. Separate provisions will be included in the Amendment for withdrawal from or liquidation of the

---

*The official title of the text is "Outline of a Facility Based on Special Drawing Rights in the Fund," (IMF Press Release of September 11, 1967).

the Special Drawing Account; Article XVI, Section 2
and Schedules D and E on withdrawal and liquidation
will continue to apply as they do at present to the
General Account of the Fund.

II. Participants and Other Holders

1. Participants. Participation in the Special
Drawing Account will be open to any member of the
Fund that undertakes the obligations of the Amend-
ment. A member's quota in the Fund will be the same
for the purposes of both the General and the Special
Drawing Accounts of the Fund.

2. Holding by General Account. The General Account will be authorized to hold and use special
drawing rights.

III. Allocation of Special Drawing Rights

1. Principles for decisions. The Special Drawing Account will allocate special drawing rights in
accordance with the provisions of the Amendment.
Special considerations applicable to the first decision to allocate special drawing rights, as well
as the principles on which all decisions to allocate
special drawing rights will be based, will be included in the introductory section of the Amendment
and, to the extent necessary, in a Report explaining
the Amendment.

2. Basic period and rate of allocation. The
following provisions will apply to any decision to
allocate special drawing rights.

i. The decision will prescribe a basic period
during which special drawing rights will be allocated
at specific intervals. The period will normally be
five years in length, but the Fund may decide that
any basic period will be of different duration. The
first basic period will begin on the effective date
of the first decision to allocate special drawing
rights.

ii. The decision will also prescribe the rate
or rates at which special drawing rights will be
allocated during the basic period. Rates will be

expressed as a percentage, uniform for all participants, of quotas on the date specified in the decision.

3.   Procedure for decision.

A.   Any decision on the basic period for, timing
of, or rate of allocation of special drawing rights
will be taken by the Board of Governors on the basis
of a proposal by the Managing Director concurred in
by the Executive Directors.

B.   Before formulating any proposal, the Managing Director after having satisfied himself that
the considerations referred to in III.1 have been
met, will conduct such consultations as will enable
him to ascertain that there is broad support among
participants for the allocation of special drawing
rights at the proposed rate and for the proposed
basic period.

C.   The Managing Director will make proposals
with respect to the allocation of special drawing
rights: (i) within sufficient time before the end
of a basic period; (ii) in the circumstances of
III.4; (iii) within six months after the Board of
Governors or the Executive Directors request that
he make a proposal. The Managing Director will make
a proposal for the first basic period when he is of
the opinion that there is broad support among the
participants to start the allocation of special drawing rights.

D.   The Executive Directors will review both the
operations of the Special Drawing Account and the
adequacy of global reserves as part of their annual
report to the Board of Governors.

4.   Change in rate of allocation or basic period.
If there are unexpected major developments which make
it desirable to change the rate at which further
special drawing rights are to be allocated for a
basic period, (i) the rate may be increased or de-
creased, or (ii) the basic period may be terminated
and a different rate of allocation adopted for a new
basic period. Paragraph III.3 will apply to such
changes.

5. Voting majority.

A. For decisions on the basic period for, timing of, amount and rate of allocation of special drawing rights, an 85 percent majority of the voting power of participants shall be required.

B. Notwithstanding A above, the decisions to decrease the rate of allocation of special drawing rights for the remainder of the basic period will be taken by a simple majority of the voting power of participants.

6. Opting out. The Amendment will include provisions that will prescribe to what extent a participant will be required initially to receive special drawing rights, but will stipulate that beyond any such amount a participant that does not vote in favor of a decision to allocate a special drawing rights may elect not to receive them under that decision.

IV. Cancellation of Special Drawing Rights

The principles set forth in III relating to the procedure and voting for the allocation of special drawing rights will be applicable, with appropriate modifications, to the cancellation of such rights.

V. Use of Special Drawing Rights

1. Right to use special drawing rights.

A. A participant will be entitled, in accordance with the provisions of V, to use special drawing rights to acquire an equivalent amount of a currency convertible in fact. A participant which thus provides currency will receive an equivalent amount of special drawing rights.

B. Within the framework of such rules and regulations as the Fund may adopt, a participant may obtain the currencies referred to in A either directly from another participant or through the Special Drawing Account.

C. Except as indicated in V.3.C, a participant will be expected to use its special drawing rights only for balance of payments needs or in the light

of developments in its total reserves and not for the
sole purpose of changing the composition of its reserves.

D.   The use of special drawing rights will not be
subject to prior challenge on the basis of this expectation, but the Fund may make representations to
any participant which, in the Fund's judgment, has
failed to observe the expectation, and may direct
drawings to such participant to the extent of such
failure.

2.   <u>Provisions of currency</u>.   A participant's obligation to provide currency will not extend beyond
a point at which its holdings of special drawing
rights in excess of the net cumulative amount of
such rights allocated to it are equal to twice that
amount.   However, a participant may provide currency,
or agree with the Fund to provide currency, in excess of this limit.

3.   <u>Selection of participants to be drawn upon</u>.
The Fund's rules and instructions relating to the
participants from which currencies should be acquired
by users of special drawing rights will be based on
the following main general principles, supplemented
by such principles as the Fund may find desirable
from time to time:

A.   Normally, currencies will be acquired from
participants that have a sufficiently strong balance
of payments and reserve position, but this will not
preclude the possibility that currency will be acquired from participants with strong reserve positions even though they have moderate balance of
payments deficits.

B.   The Fund's primary criterion will be to seek
to approach over time equality, among the participants indicated from time to time by the criteria
in A above, in the ratios of their holdings of special drawing rights, or such holdings in excess of
net cumulative allocations thereof, to total reserves.

C.   In addition, the Fund will, in its rules and
instructions, provide for such use of special drawing
rights, either directly between participants or
through the intermediary of the Special Drawing Account, as will promote voluntary reconstitution and
reconstitution under V.4.

D.   Subject to the provisions of V.1.C, a participant may use its special drawing rights to purchase
balances of its currency held by another participant,
with the agreement of the latter.

4.   Reconstitution.

A.   Members that use their special drawing rights
will incur an obligation to reconstitute their position in accordance with principles which will take
account of the amount and the duration of the use.
These principles will be laid down in rules and regulations of the Fund.

B.   The rules for reconstitution of drawings
made during the first basic period will be based on
the following principles:

i.   The average net use, taking into account
both use below and holdings above its net cumulative
allocation, made by a participant of its special
drawing rights calculated on the basis of the preceding five years, shall not exceed 70 percent of
its average net cumulative allocation during this
period.   Reconstitution under this subparagraph i
will be brought about through the mechanism of transfers, by the Fund directing drawings correspondingly.

ii. Participants will pay due regard to the
desirability of pursuing over time a balanced relationship between their holdings of special drawing
rights and other reserves.

C.   Reconstitution rules will be reviewed before
the end of the first and of each subsequent period
and new rules will be adopted, if necessary.   If
new rules are not adopted for a basic period, the
rules for the preceding period shall apply unless
it is decided to abrogate reconstitution rules.   The
same majority as is required for decisions on the
basic period, timing of, or rate of allocation of
special drawing rights will be required for decisions to adopt, amend, or abrogate reconstitution
of drawings made after the effective date of the
amendment, unless otherwise decided.

VI.   Interest and Maintenance of Gold Value

A.   Interest.   A moderate rate of interest will
be paid in special drawing rights on holdings of

special drawing rights. The cost of this interest
will be assessed against all participants in proportion to net cumulative allocations of special
drawing rights to them.

B. <u>Maintenance of gold value</u>. The unit of value
for expressing special drawing rights will be equal
to 0.888 671 grams of fine gold. The rights and obligations of participants and of the Special Drawing
Account will be subject to an absolute maintenance
of gold value or to provisions similar to Article
IV, Section 8 of the Fund's Articles.

VII. Functions of Fund Organs and Voting

1. <u>Exercise of powers</u>. The decisions taken
with respect to the Special Drawing Account, and
the supervision of its operations, will be carried
out by the Board of Governors, the Executive Directors, the Managing Director, and the staff of the
Fund. Certain powers, and in particular those relating to the adoption of decisions concerning the
allocation, cancellation, and certain aspects of
the use of special drawing rights, will be reserved
to the Board of Governors. All other powers, except
those specifically granted to other organs, will be
vested in the Board of Governors which will be able
to delegate them to the Executive Directors.

2. <u>Voting</u>. Except as otherwise provided in the
Amendment, all decisions pertaining to the Special
Drawing Account will be taken by a majority of votes
cast. The precise formula for the voting power of
participants, which will include basic and weighted
votes, and possibly the adjustment of voting power
in relation to the use of special drawing rights,
will be the subject of later consideration.

VIII. General Provisions

1. <u>Collaboration</u>. Participants will undertake
to collaborate with the Fund in order to facilitate
the proper functioning and effective use of special
drawing rights within the international monetary
system.

2. <u>Nonfulfillment of obligations</u>.

A. If the Fund finds that a participant has failed to fulfill its obligations to provide currency in accordance with the Amendment, the Fund may suspend the right of the participant to use its special drawing right.

B. If the Fund finds that a participant has failed to fulfill any other obligation under the Amendment, the Fund may suspend the participant's right to use any special drawing rights allocated to, or acquired by, it after the suspension.

C. Suspension under A or B above will not affect a participant's obligation to provide currency in accordance with the Amendment.

D. The Fund may at any time terminate a suspension under A or B above.

3. Accounts. All changes in holdings of special drawing rights will take effect when recorded in the accounts of the Special Drawing Account.

IX. Entry into Force

The Amendment would enter into force in accordance with the terms of Article XVII of the Fund's Articles.

[Note: The full text of the Amendment to its Articles of Agreement is available from the International Monetary Fund, Washington, D.C., 20431.]

BIBLIOGRAPHY

BIBLIOGRAPHY

Books

Aliber, Robert Z. The Future of the Dollar as an
    International Currency. New York: Frederick
    A. Praeger, Publishers, 1966.

Aron, Raymond. Peace and War. New York: Double-
    day, 1966.

Barnet, Richard J., and Marcus Raskin. After Twenty
    Years, the Decline of NATO. New York: Vintage
    Books, 1966.

Cassell, Francis. Gold or Credit. New York: Fred-
    erick A. Praeger, Publishers, 1965.

Cleveland, Harold van B. The Atlantic Idea and Its
    European Rivals. New York: McGraw Hill, 1966.

Cooper, Richard N. The Economics of Interdependence.
    New York: McGraw Hill, 1968.

Grubel, Herbert G., ed. World Monetary Reform:
    Plans and Issues. Stanford: Stanford Univer-
    sity Press, 1963.

Harrod, Sir Roy. Reforming the World's Money. New
    York: St. Martin's Press, 1965.

Hess, John L. The Case for De Gaulle. New York:
    William Morrow, 1968.

Hinshaw, Randall, ed. Monetary Reform and the Price
    of Gold: Alternative Approaches. Baltimore:
    Johns Hopkins Press, 1967.

Hoffmann, Stanley. Gulliver's Troubles, or the Set-
    ting of American Foreign Policy. New York:
    McGraw Hill, 1968.

189

Johnson, Harry G. Economic Policies Toward Less Developed Countries. Washington, D.C.: The Brookings Institution, 1967.

Kissinger, Henry A. The Troubled Partnership. New York: Anchor Books, 1966.

Lerche, Charles O., and Abdul A. Said. Concepts of International Politics. Englewood Cliffs, N.J.: Prentice-Hall, 1963.

Machlup, Fritz, ed. International Payments, Debts, and Gold: Collected Essays. New York: Charles Scribner's Sons, 1964.

_____. Remaking the International Monetary System. Baltimore: The Johns Hopkins Press, 1968.

Morgenstern, Oskar. The Limits of Economics. London: William Hodge and Company, Limited, 1937.

Morgenthau, Hans. Politics Among Nations. New York: Alfred A. Knopf, 1959.

_____. Scientific Man Versus Power Politics. Chicago: University of Chicago Press, 1946.

Rolfe, Sidney E. Gold and World Power. New York: Harper and Row, 1966.

Roosa, Robert V. The Dollar and World Liquidity. New York: Random House, 1967.

_____. Monetary Reform for the World Economy. New York: Harper and Row, 1965.

Servan-Schreiber, J. J. The American Challenge. New York: Atheneum, 1968.

Steel, Ronald. The End of Alliance. New York: Delta Books, 1966.

_____. Pax Americana. New York: Viking Press, 1967.

Triffin, Robert. Gold and the Dollar Crisis. New Haven: Yale University Press, 1961.

_____. Our International Monetary System: Yesterday, Today, and Tomorrow. New York: Random House, 1968.

_____. The World Money Maze. New Haven: Yale
    University Press, 1966.

Wilcox, Francis O., and H. Field Haviland, Jr., eds.
    The Atlantic Community, Progress and Prospects.
    New York: Frederick A. Praeger, Publishers,
    1963.

Yeager, Leland. International Monetary Relations.
    New York: Harper and Row, 1966.

Young, John Parke. The International Economy. New
    York: The Ronald Press Company, 1963.

                    Official Publications

Banca D'Italia. Abridged Version of the Report for
    the Year 1966. Rome, 1967.

Bank for International Settlements. Thirty-Eighth
    Annual Report. Basle, Switzerland, 1968.

_____. "Press Review," January, 1965-September,
    1967.

Blessing, Karl. "Capitalism and World Monetary
    Problems," Deutsche Bundesbank, Auszuge Aus
    Presseartikeln, September 21, 1966.

_____. "Comments on the International Monetary
    Situation," October 4, 1965. (Mimeographed.)

Board of Governors of the Federal Reserve System.
    Federal Reserve Bulletin. 1958-69.

Daane, J. Dewey. International Liquidity, A Contri-
    bution to the Dialogue. Washington, D.C.:
    Federal Reserve System, 1965.

Debre, Michel. "The International Monetary System,"
    Press Release of the French Embassy, January
    13, 1967.

De Gaulle, Charles. "Excerpts from Press Conference
    of February 4, 1965." Press Release of the
    French Embassy, February 5, 1965.

Deming, Frederick L. "The Quest for Liquidity."
    U.S. Treasury Department Press Release, Septem-
    ber 16, 1967.

_____. "Updating Our International Monetary Sys-
tem." U.S. Treasury Department Press Release,
February 16, 1966.

Deutsche Bundesbank. Auszuge Aus Presseartikeln
[Press Summary], October, 1963-September, 1969.

Economic Report of the President: 1966. Washington, D.C.: U.S. Government Printing Office,
1966.

Emminger, Dr. Otmar. "How Urgent is Reform of the
International Monetary System?" Translated
in an unclassified U.S. State Department Air-
gram, September 3, 1966.

_____. "International Monetary Reform." Deutsche
Bundesbank Press Release, September 11, 1967.

Fowler, Henry H. "1966--Year of Decision and Opportunity for International Economic Cooperation."
U.S. Treasury Department Press Release, May 27,
1966.

_____. "Remarks before the Virginia State Bar
Association," U.S. Treasury Department Press
Release, July 11, 1965.

_____. "A World Monetary System for a Greater
Society of Nations." U.S. Treasury Department
Press Release, March 17, 1967.

Giscard d'Estaing, Valery. International Monetary
Problems. Paris: L'Economie, 1965.

Group of Ten. Communiqué of Ministers and Governors
and Report of Deputies. 1966.

_____. Communiqués of Ministerial Meetings.
October, 1963-October, 1969.

_____. Report of the Study Group on the Creation
of Reserve Assets. 1965.

_____. Statement by Ministers of the Group of
Ten and Annex Prepared by Their Deputies. 1964.

Inter-American Committee on the Alliance for Progress.
International Monetary Reform and Latin America.
Washington, D.C.: Pan American Union, 1966.

BIBLIOGRAPHY   193

International Monetary Fund. Annual Report. Wash-
     ington, D.C.: The Fund, 1963-69.

_____. Articles of Agreement of the International
Monetary Fund. Washington, D.C.: The Fund,
1967.

_____. International Financial News Survey.
Washington, D.C.: The Fund, 1967-69.

_____. Morning Press. Washington, D.C.: The
Fund, December, 1963-April, 1968.

_____. "Outline of a Facility Based on Special
Drawing Rights in the Fund." Washington, D.C.:
The Fund, Press Release of September 11, 1967.

_____. Proposed Amendments of Articles of Agree-
ment. Washington, D.C.: The Fund, April, 1968.

_____. Summary Proceedings of Annual Meetings.
Washington, D.C.: The Fund, 1962-68.

_____. Transcripts of Press Conferences Conducted
by Pierre-Paul Schweitzer, Managing Director of
the Fund, and Otmar Emminger, Chairman of the
Deputies of the Group of Ten, November 30, 1966,
January 26, 1967, April 16, 1967 and June 21,
1967. Washington, D.C.: The Fund.

International Monetary Reform. London: British
     Information Services, 1967.

Javits, Jacob K. "International Monetary Reform:
     Vital U.S. Objective." Washington, D.C.: Press
     Release of Senator Javits' Office, October 26,
     1964.

The Monetary Committee of the European Economic Com-
     munity. Tenth Report on the Activities of the
     Monetary Committee. Brussels, 1968.

National Advisory Council on International Monetary
     and Financial Policies. Special Report on the
     Proposed Amendment of the Articles of Agreement
     of the International Monetary Fund. Washington,
     D.C.: U.S. Government Printing Office, 1968.

Polak, J. J. "Special Drawing Rights," Finance and
     Development, IV (December, 1967), 275-80.

"Special Drawing Rights: A Major Step in the Evolu-
     tion of the World's Monetary System," Federal
     Reserve Bank of New York Monthly Review, L
     (January, 1968), 10-13.

United Nations Conference on Trade and Development.
     International Monetary Issues and the Developing
     Countries. New York, November 1, 1965.

U.S. Congress, House of Representatives, Committee
     on Banking and Currency. The International
     Monetary Fund's Special Drawing Rights Proposal
     and the Current International Financial Situa-
     tion. Subcommittee Hearings. 90th Cong., 2nd
     Sess., April 12, 1968.

_____. Special Drawing Rights. Committee Report
     on H.R. 16911, 90th Cong., 2nd Sess., May 6,
     1968.

_____. Statement of International Finance Sub-
     committee House Committee on Banking and Cur-
     rency, on the August 10, 1964, Recommendations
     of "Group of Ten" on the International Monetary
     System. Committee Press Release, August 21,
     1964.

_____. To Establish a Facility Based on Special
     Drawing Rights in the International Monetary
     Fund. Hearings. 90th Cong., 2nd Sess., on
     H.R. 16911, May 1-2, 1968.

U.S. Congress, Joint Economic Committee. Contingency
     Planning for U.S. International Monetary Policy.
     Papers submitted to Subcommittee, 89th Cong.,
     2nd Sess., December, 1966. Washington, D.C.:
     U.S. Government Printing Office, 1966.

_____. The Future of U.S. Foreign Trade Policy.
     Subcommittee Hearings. 90th Cong., 1st Sess.,
     July 11-20, 1967, Vol. I. Washington, D.C.:
     U.S. Government Printing Office, 1967.

_____. Guidelines for International Monetary
     Reform. Subcommittee Hearings. 89th Cong.,
     1st Sess., July 27-29, 1965, Part 1--Hearings
     and Part 2--Supplement. Washington, D.C.:
     U.S. Government Printing Office, 1965.

_____. Guidelines for Improving the International Monetary System. Subcommittee Report on International Exchange and Payments. 89th Cong., 1st Sess., August, 1965. Washington, D.C.: U.S. Government Printing Office, 1965.

_____. Guidelines for Improving the International Monetary System--Round Two. Subcommittee Report on International Exchange and Payments. 90th Cong., 1st Sess., December, 1967. Washington, D.C.: U.S. Government Printing Office, 1967.

_____. New Plan for International Monetary Reserves. Subcommittee Hearings. 90th Cong., 1st Sess., September 14, and November 22, 1967, Parts 1 and 2. Washington, D.C.: U.S. Government Printing Office, 1967.

U.S. Congress, Senate, Committee on Banking and Currency. Balance of Payments--1965. Subcommittee Hearings. 89th Cong., 1st Sess., March, 1965, Part 1. Washington, D.C.: U.S. Government Printing Office, 1965.

_____. Gold Cover. Hearings. 90th Cong., 2nd Sess., on S.1307, S.2815, and S.2857, January 30-31 and February 1, 1968. Washington, D.C.: U.S. Government Printing Office, 1968.

U.S. Department of Commerce. Survey of Current Business. Washington, D.C.: U.S. Government Printing Office, January, 1966-July, 1969.

U.S. Treasury Department. Maintaining the Strength of the United States Dollar in a Strong Free World Economy. Washington, D.C.: U.S. Government Printing Office, 1968.

_____. Summary of the Report of the Group of Ten Deputies. Washington, D.C.: Press Release, August 25, 1966.

_____. Transcripts of press conferences of Henry H. Fowler, Secretary of the Treasury. September 14, 1965 and July 27, 1966.

_____. Transcript of press conference of Otmar Emminger, April 22, 1966.

Willis, George H., and Fred L. Springborn. The Need
    for International Reserves. Washington, D.C.:
    U.S. Treasury Department, 1967.

Working Party No. 3, Economic Policy Committee of
    the Organization for Economic Cooperation and
    Development. The Balance of Payments Adjustment
    Process. Paris: Organization for Economic Co-
    operation and Development, August, 1966.

                Pamphlets and Periodicals

"Alarmed Voice of a New Europe," Life, LXIV (May 17,
    1968), 41-50.

Albrook, Robert C. "Secreatry Fowler's Crusade for
    Monetary Reform," Fortune, LXXVI (August, 1967),
    78-150.

Aliber, Robert Z. "The Management of the Dollar in
    International Finance." Essays in International
    Finance, No. 13. Princeton: Princeton Univer-
    sity Press, 1964.

Altman, Oscar L. "The Management of International
    Liquidity," IMF Staff Papers, XI, 216-47.

Aron, Raymond. "Is the European Idea Dying?" The
    Atlantic Community Quarterly, V (Spring, 1967),
    37-47.

Aschinger, F. E. "The French Monetary Campaign,"
    Swiss Review of World Affairs, XV (July, 1965),
    13-15.

_____. "The General Revision of the IMF," The
    Banker, CXVII (January, 1968), 28-33.

Aubrey, Henry G. "Behind the Veil of International
    Money." Essays in International Finance, No.
    71. Princeton: Princeton University Press,
    1969.

_____. "The Political Economy of International
    Monetary Reform," Social Research, XXXIII
    (Summer, 1966), 218-54.

Baffi, Paolo. "Western European Inflation and the
    Reserve Currencies," Banca Nazionale Del Lavoro
    Quarterly Review, XXI (March, 1968), 3-22.

Bator, Francis M. "International Liquidity: An
    Unofficial View of the United States Case,"
    American Economic Association, Papers and Pro-
    ceedings, LVIII (May, 1968), 620-24.

Bergsten, C. Fred. "Taking the Monetary Initiative,"
    Foreign Affairs, XLVI (July, 1968), 713-32.

"Better Than Nothing," The Economist, CCXXIX (July 8,
    1967), 138.

Birnbaum, Eugene A. "Gold and the International
    Monetary System: An Orderly Reform." Essays
    in International Finance, No. 66. Princeton:
    Princeton University Press, 1968.

Blessing, Karl. "International Monetary Problems,"
    Progress, LI (April, 1966), 138-44.

Bratter, Herbert. "Stepping Stones to Rio," Banking,
    LX (September, 1967), 40-43.

"Cards on the Table," The Economist, CCXVIII (Feb-
    ruary 5, 1966), 536.

Clarke, William M. "What the General Meant About
    Gold," Westminster Bank Review (May, 1965),
    2-13.

Cleveland, Harold van B. "The International Mone-
    tary System Muddles Through," Columbia Journal
    of World Business, IV (January-February, 1969),
    19-24.

"A Cure Worse Than the Disease," The Economist,
    CCXV (February 6, 1965), 567-69.

Despres, Emile, Charles P. Kindleberger, and Walter
    S. Salant. "The Dollar and World Liquidity--
    A World View," The Economist, CCXVIII (Feb-
    ruary 5, 1966), 526-29.

EMB (Ltd.) "Gold, Reserves, and the International
    Monetary System." Unpublished paper, July 26,
    1967.

"The Emminger Compromise," The Economist, CCXVIII
    (January 29, 1966), 430.

Fabra, Paul. "The Moneymen of France," Interplay,
    I (January, 1968), 37-40.

"From Munich to Rio," Common Market, VII (June,
    1967), 174-76.

"The General Says No," The Economist, CCXVIII (March
    5, 1966), 924.

Halm, George N. "International Financial Intermedi-
    ation: Deficits Benign and Malignant." Essays
    in International Finance, No. 68. Princeton:
    Princeton University Press, 1968.

Hawkins, Robert G. "Compendium of Plans for Inter-
    national Monetary Reform." Bulletin No. 37-38,
    C. J. Devine Institute of Finance, Graduate
    School of Business Administration, New York
    University (December, 1965).

Hawkins, Robert G., and Sidney E. Rolfe. "A Criti-
    cal Survey of Plans for International Monetary
    Reform." Bulletin No. 36, C. J. Devine Insti-
    tute of Finance, Graduate School of Business
    Administration, New York University (November,
    1965).

"Impasse on Liquidity," The Banker, CXVI (April,
    1966), 215-18.

"Inflation and Economic Policy." Distributed by
    Model, Roland, and Company, Inc., September,
    1966.

"Interview: Michel Debre," The Banker, CXVII
    (February, 1967), 102-08.

"Interview: Henry Fowler," The Banker, CXVII
    (June, 1967), 472-85.

Jay, Peter. "Why France Balks," Interplay, I
    (December, 1967), 36-40.

Kindleberger, Charles P. "The Politics of Inter-
    national Money and World Language." Essays
    in International Finance, No. 61. Princeton:
    Princeton University Press, 1967.

Kissinger, Henry A. "Central Issues of American
    Foreign Policy." Agenda for the Nation. Ed-
    ited by Kermit Gordon. Washington, D.C.:
    The Brookings Institution, 1968. Pp. 585-614.

"Liquidity: Advancing Unhappily," The Economist,
     CCXX (July 30, 1966), 460-61.

"Liquidity at the Crossroads," The Banker, CXV (No-
     vember, 1965), 707-10.

"Liquidity: The Golden Punchline," The Economist,
     CCXXI (December 3, 1966), 1056-57.

Machlup, Fritz. "The Need for Monetary Reserves,"
     Banca Nazionale Del Lavoro Quarterly Review,
     XIX (September, 1966), 175-222.

_____. "World Monetary Debate--Bases for Agree-
     ment," The Banker, CXVI (September, 1966),
     598-611.

"Mr. Fowler's Surprise," The Economist, CCXVI (July
     17, 1965), 261.

"New Twist to the Laocoon," The Economist, CCXXII
     (January 21, 1967), 243.

"Nine Out of Ten?" The Economist, CCXIX (March 12,
     1966), 1028.

Oetking, Robert. "Britain's Common Market Bid and
     World Monetary Reform," Bankers Monthly Magazine,
     LXXXIV (June 15, 1967), 22-23.

Ossola, Rinaldo. "On the Creation of New Reserve
     Assets: The Report of the Study Group of Ten,"
     Banca Nazionale Del Lavoro Quarterly Review,
     XVIII (September, 1965), 272-92.

_____. "Progress of Discussions on Monetary Re-
     form," Review of the Economic Conditions in
     Italy (January, 1967), 7-13.

"Paths of Dalliance," The Economist, CCXI (May 2,
     1964), 461-63.

Polak, J. J. "The New Facility in the IMF," The
     Banker, CXVII (November, 1967), 964-71.

Roosa, Robert V., and Fred Hirsch. "Reserves, Re-
     serve Currencies, and Vehicle Currencies: An
     Argument." Essays in International Finance,
     No. 54. Princeton: Princeton University Press,
     1966.

Rueff, Jacques, and Fred Hirsch. "The Role and the
    Rule of Gold: An Argument." Essays in Inter-
    national Finance, No. 47. Princeton: Prince-
    ton University Press, 1965.

Salant, Walter S. Does the International Monetary
    System Need Reform? Washington, D.C.: The
    Brookings Institution, 1964.

Schmitt, Hans O. "Political Conditions for Inter-
    national Currency Reform," International Organi-
    zation, XXVI (Summer, 1964), 543-57.

"SDRs in Shape," The Economist, CCXXXII (April 27,
    1968), 71.

Shonfield, Andrew. "Towards an International Cur-
    rency," International Affairs, XLIII (January,
    1967), 39-50.

Tobin, James. "Europe and the Dollar," The Review
    of Economics and Statistics, XLVI (May, 1964),
    123-26.

"Tokyo's Emerging Agenda," The Economist, CCXI
    (May 2, 1964), 514.

Triffin, Robert. "The Balance of Payments and the
    Foreign Investment Position of the United
    States." Essays in International Finance, No.
    55. Princeton: Princeton University Press,
    1966.

_____. "International Monetary Reform," Economic
    Bulletin for Latin America, XI (April, 1966),
    10-41.

_____. "Will 1965 Repeat 1931?" The Reporter,
    XXXII (April 8, 1965), 27-30.

"U.S. Pounds the Desk on Monetary Reform," Business
    Week (April 29, 1967), 132-34.

White, A. N. "International Monetary Reform: Prob-
    lems and Progress," Westminster Bank Review
    (November, 1966), 45-56.

"Will Unreason Win?" The Economist, CCXXIII (April
    22, 1967), 365-66.

Newspapers

American Banker, January, 1966-April, 1968.

Europe (Daily Bulletin of the Agence Internationale
        D'Information pour la Presse, Luxembourg and
        Brussels), September, 1966-July, 1967.

The Financial Times (London), January, 1966-April,
        1968.

The Journal of Commerce, December, 1963-April, 1968.

Le Monde (Paris), January, 1965-April, 1968.

The New York Times, December, 1963-October, 1969.

The Times (London), January, 1964-December, 1967.

The Wall Street Journal, January, 1964-October, 1969.

The Washington Post, January, 1964-October, 1969.

ABOUT THE AUTHOR

Stephen D. Cohen is Chief Economist for the United States-Japan Trade Council in Washington, D.C., where he has responsibility for studying and reporting on all aspects of U.S. foreign economic policy.

He was able to observe U.S.-European political and economic relations in his previous position as assistant to the vice president for European affairs in the International Division of the Philadelphia National Bank. Prior to that, Dr. Cohen spent three years as an international economist in the U.S. Treasury Department's Office of International Affairs, where he served as a country desk officer for several European countries and also as a coordinator for efforts to utilize U.S. Government-owned foreign currencies to the maximum extent possible as a balance-of-payments savings.

Dr. Cohen received his Ph.D. from the American University's School of International Service in Washington, D.C.